Grill!

Grill!

Quick and delicious recipes for indoor and outdoor grilling

Pippa Cuthbert &
Lindsay Cameron Wilson

Intercourse, PA 17534
800/762-7171
www.GoodBks.com

Dedication: To our fathers, Ian and Gordon

First published in North America by
Good Books
Intercourse, PA 17534
800/762-7171
www.GoodBks.com

Text and recipe copyright © 2006 Pippa Cuthbert and Lindsay Cameron Wilson
Photographs copyright © 2006 New Holland Publishers (UK) Ltd
Copyright © 2006 New Holland Publishers (UK) Ltd

GRILL!
Good Books, Intercourse, PA 17534
International Standard Book Number: 978-1-56148-518-5; 1-56148-518-7 (paperback edition)
International Standard Book Number: 978-1-56148-519-2; 1-56148-519-5 (comb-bound edition)

Library of Congress Catalog Card Number: 2005030600

Library of Congress Cataloging-in-Publication Data:

Cuthbert, Pippa.
     Grill! : quick and delicious recipes for indoor and outdoor grilling / Pippa Cuthbert & Lindsay Cameron Wilson.
          p. cm.
Includes bibliographical references and index.
     ISBN 978-1-56148-518-5 (pbk) -- ISBN 978-1-56148-519-2 (comb)
     ISBN 1-56148-518-7 (pbk.) -- ISBN 1-56148-519-5 (comb)
1. Barbecue cookery. I. Wilson, Lindsay Cameron. II. Title.
   TX840.B3C88 2006
   641.5'784--dc22
                    2005030600

Senior Editor: Clare Hubbard
Editor: Anna Bennett
Design: Paul Wright
Photography: Stuart West
Food styling: Pippa Cuthbert and Lindsay Cameron Wilson
Production: Hazel Kirkman
Editorial Direction: Rosemary Wilkinson

Reproduction by Pica Digital PTE Ltd, Singapore
Printed and bound in China by C&C Offset Printing Co., Ltd.

Acknowledgements

Many thanks, as always, to Camilla Schneideman at Divertimenti (www.divertimenti.co.uk) and Lindy Wiffen at Ceramica Blue (www.ceramicablue.co.uk) for their friendship and gorgeous props. Thanks also to our discerning tasters and testers, especially Cynthia Shupe, for her hard work and precision. And to Greg Deal, butcher at Pete's Frootique in Halifax, for answering countless questions! Many thanks also to all our family and friends who have shared numerous good times around the grill and many inspirational recipes and ideas with us. Thanks to Annabelle Judd for the use of her beautiful garden for the photoshoot. And finally, thanks to Rosie and Eric and all the team at Books for Cooks for their continued support.

Both metric and imperial measures are given for the recipes – follow either set of measures, but not a mixture of both as they are not interchangeable.
All herbs used are fresh unless otherwise stated.

NOTE

The author and publishers have made every effort to ensure that all instructions given in this book are safe and accurate, but they cannot accept liability for any resulting injury or loss or damage to either property or person, whether direct or consequential and howsoever arising.

Contents

Introduction

This is a book about grilling, not just about barbecue.

Let me explain. I spent some time living in the American South, where barbecue is a noun, not a verb. By American definition, barbecue is a tough cut of meat cooked slowly over a wood-fired grill. The meat is basted with a simple vinegar- or sometimes tomato-based sauce. The result is meltingly tender, smoke-infused meat. But, if I can generalize, where there's smoke, there's fire. And where there's fire, there are men. And where there are men, there's competition. In America, whole states, cities, neighborhoods and families are divided by *barbecue*. Take North Carolina, for example. Texas generally unites behind beef brisket, South Carolina is devoted to its mustard-based pork, while Kansas City loves its ribs. In North Carolina, however, things aren't so simple. On the western side of the state (Lexington or Piedmont), barbecue means a hog shoulder basted with a red, tomato-based sauce. Over in the east, on the other hand, they follow the old, North Carolina adage – use every part of the pig except

for the squeal – with a little vinegar-based sauce to help it along. Both claim to have the best barbecue, and neither will budge. This debate isn't new; it is a controversy that has been simmering away for years, but recently there was a major development. In the spring of 2005 a city bylaw was passed naming Lexington, with its pork shoulder and tomato-based sauce, the "Barbecue Capital of the World." Vinegar purists were up in arms. Friendships died, fists were drawn and reporters gathered. I caught the breaking news in my kitchen in Halifax, Nova Scotia, as I innocently prepared a marinade for my pork ribs. I was listening to a North America-wide live radio program, and I could feel the heat right through the radio.

At least the people of North Carolina agree on one thing – the use of the word "barbecue." Roger Dennis, a North Carolina newspaper columnist and barbecue devotee, set his readers straight when he wrote the following: "Barbecue – for the thousandth time – is a noun. It is not a verb or an adjective. You cook a pig and you get barbecue. You grill steaks and burgers. You do not 'barbecue' anything. So shut up about it."

We're passionate about cooking anything alfresco. We love the way aromas waft through the garden, calling guests to gather by the flame. We crave the effects of a smoky charcoal, especially when accompanied by a handful of aromatic wood chips. We appreciate the ease and immediacy of a gas grill, and value the versatility of the grill pan. They all capture the essence of casual dining, regardless of the weather, the season, or the time of the day. We're girls who are devoted to the grill. With this devotion comes strength and wisdom. We are strong enough to grill with the guys, but wise enough to avoid the competition that shrouds all things "barbecue."

We're not certain why competition follows flame. Maybe it's the primal action of meat to fire. Perhaps it's the over-sized tools. Regardless of reason, grilling not only tears up towns, it divides friends. When

Pippa and her friends get together for barbecues in New Zealand, the guys elbow their way to the grill with beer and raw steaks in hand, while the women casually toss salads and sip wine in the kitchen. Thousands of kilometers away in Halifax, Nova Scotia, you'll find exactly the same scenario in my back garden. But history, as they say, is meant to be broken. Women can grill, men can make salads, and anyone can turn a noun into a verb.

The word barbecue is much older than the dish. The Tainos (a Haitian tribe obliterated by European explorers) used the word *barbacoa* to describe a framework of sticks used for sleeping on or cooking over. The word was borrowed by the Spanish, and worked its way into the English language as *barbecue* at the end of the seventeenth century, still referring to a wooden framework. By the early eighteenth century, *barbecue* was exclusively a device upon which to roast meat; by the end of that century, its meaning was extended to any dish that was cooked upon such a device.

Many say the word derives from the French *barbe à queue*, literally "beard to tail," referring to the practice of spit-roasting whole animals. Regardless of provenance, however, it's safe to say that the word "barbecue" has had a checkered semantic history. But we're laid-back women – we don't care whether we grill, barbecue, or barbecue "barbecue." What we do care about is taste. Flavor. Fresh ingredients. Global influences. Straightforward methods. Casual gatherings. Friends. Family. And, most of all, the relaxed feeling that only comes from cooking food over fire.

Most of our recipes are interchangeable from pan to grill, depending on mood, weather, or whatever is at hand. We have indicated, however, when one or the other is advisable. There are certain recipes, for example, that can only be cooked on the grill. After all roasting a chicken on a beer can just wouldn't work in a grill pan!

 Grill only

 Grill pan only

Successful grilling

Grilling can be a breeze if you follow our simple guidelines. Successful grilling calls for thought and planning: remember to think like a scout and BE PREPARED. How often have you sunk your teeth into a suspiciously pink chicken leg or been served a slightly over-charred sausage? These all too common occurrences can be easily avoided if you follow our easy instructions. Our marinating and food safety tips apply as much to indoor grilling as they do to outdoor cooking.

Marinating tips

■ For mess-free marinating and an even, all-over coating, place your marinade ingredients in a strong plastic bag. If you have no large plastic bags or you are marinating meat on skewers, then always use non-corrosive dishes such as Pyrex, glass or stainless steel and cover tightly with plastic wrap to avoid other foods tainting the flavor.
■ If you are marinating your meat for longer then 30 minutes, always do so in the fridge. Remove it only 30 minutes before cooking to bring it back to room temperature.

■ In some recipes we heat the marinade. This speeds up the marinating time. Do not, however, heat marinades containing milk products such as yogurt and do not use hot marinades on fish, because they will begin to cook it immediately on contact. Hot, not boiling, marinades should be poured over the meat and left for no longer than 30 minutes at room temperature just prior to cooking.
■ Never mix raw foods such as fish and chicken in the same marinade – for maximum safety, keep foods separate.
■ Never combine cooked meat with your uncooked marinade. Instead, use the uncooked marinade during cooking for basting the meat.

■ If your marinade has a high sugar content it will burn more easily. Always hold off basting with these marinades until at least halfway through cooking. Always ensure that the last basting has had sufficient cooking. A low-sugar content marinade can be used to baste the meat from the start of cooking.

■ Before placing marinated items on the grill shake off any excess marinade, particularly if there is oil in it, to prevent flaring and burning.

■ Never use your best extra virgin olive oil in a marinade. It will burn and smoke because of the high content of monounsaturated fatty acids. Use light olive oil or vegetable oil instead, and save your best extra virgin olive oil for salad dressings.

■ Acids are an important ingredient in marinades as they help break down enzymes and tenderize the meat. Common acid ingredients found in marinades are lemon juice, yogurt, wine, soy sauce and vinegar. Some fruits such as kiwi fruit and pomegranate are also highly acidic and are common meat tenderizers.

■ Do not over-marinate your meat. You may gain in flavor by doing this but you will also lose in texture. Some acidic marinades will break down the meat or fish if left too long.

Food safety and hygiene

Food safety is an important issue when it comes to grilling, keeping in mind that it is usually a hot summer's day when the grill comes out. When you're grilling, the greatest risk of food poisoning comes from raw and undercooked meats. Bugs such as E.coli, salmonella and campylobacter can cause serious illness. Follow these simple steps to avoid illness:

■ Always wash your hands thoroughly before and after handling raw meats.

■ Always keep your food cool, covered and out of the reach of animals and children.

■ All meats should be thoroughly defrosted before cooking. The best way to do this is to defrost them in the fridge overnight.

■ All marinated foods should be refrigerated until about 30 minutes before cooking unless a hot marinade has been used (see page 10). Take chicken out no longer than 30 minutes before cooking.

■ Use separate dishes to transfer uncooked and cooked meats and never combine the two.

■ Check that your meat is at a safe temperature for eating; insert a meat thermometer into the thickest part of the flesh so it is as close as possible to the center of the meat.

Avoid contact with bones, which will give you an inaccurate reading. The temperatures should read approximately:

Beef/lamb/venison = 140–149°F (60–65°C) for medium-rare, 158–167°F (70–75°C) for well done. The meat should feel soft but firm and should still be juicy.

Pork = 149–158°F (65–70°C). The meat should be opaque throughout but still juicy.

Chicken = the flesh should be opaque throughout with no traces of pink and the juices should run clear when a skewer is inserted into the thickest part of the flesh.

■ Don't assume that meat charred on the outside will be cooked properly on the inside. Check that the center of the food is piping hot, particularly when cooking chicken, burgers, sausages and kebabs.

■ Always have a bucket of sand nearby just in case the flames get out of hand.

TOOLS OF THE TRADE

Long tongs
These are essential for turning meats. Avoid any with sharp teeth or you will pierce the meat, and juices will be lost, causing flare-ups and tough, dry results.

Wide spatula
A useful tool when dealing with whole chickens, pizzas or any large items. Ideally a pizza paddle with a long handle will do the job best. Otherwise use a large flat fish slice with a long handle.

Clean plates and trays
Essential for cooked food. Never put cooked meats back on the same plate or dish that they came off. One trick is to line the dish of uncooked meats with plastic wrap. While the meat is cooking, remove the plastic wrap and you are left with a clean dish for the cooked meat.

Timer
An extremely useful piece of equipment to have at your side when manning the grill. Over-cooked meats are never a joy to eat, so set the timer and then you can carry on socializing. Timers are particularly useful when the lid is down and you can't see exactly what is going on.

Brushes

Essential for basting meats or vegetables as they cook. Today you can buy heatproof silicon brushes but if you can't get hold of these, just use whatever brushes you have available. If you don't have a brush, then try using a bunch of hard herbs such as thyme and rosemary to dip into the marinade and brush over the meat or vegetables. This is just as effective and imparts a delicious flavor at the same time.

Paper towels
Essential in order to keep your workspace clean. It is also useful to help absorb any meat juices when meat is resting.

Large kitchen knife
This is useful for carving large cuts of meat such as a fillet of beef or a whole chicken.

Small sharp knife

Use this to test if the meat is ready. This is particularly important for pork and chicken, where bacteria are more likely to be found and the temperature is more critical.

Thermometer

This enables you to test if your meat has reached the correct temperature (see "Food safety and hygiene," page 11).

Long matches or lighters

These enable you to light the grill easily without burning your fingers.

Cutting boards

Do not use the same boards for cooked and uncooked meats.

Wooden or bamboo skewers

These should be soaked in cold water for at least 30 minutes before cooking so they don't burn. If you have forgotten to soak your skewers, then wrap the ends in foil to prevent burning. Alternatively, use metal skewers for long-cooking foods like a whole chicken or use sugar cane, rosemary skewers or lemongrass stalks for short-cooking foods such as fish kebabs.

Poultry shears

Useful for cutting through raw chicken with bones.

Hinged wire grills

These are an easy way to cook fish over charcoal. The fish is encased, so you don't have to worry about keeping it intact while turning it.

Drip pan

Use disposable aluminium trays or an old roasting dish that you don't mind ruining. Place it over the coals and under the grill when grilling particularly fatty meats or meats in marinades that contain a lot of oil. It will catch the drips and help prevent flaring and burning.

Smoke chip box

Various kinds of smoke chip boxes are available, from stainless steel to cast iron to makeshift foil packages.

They fit inside gas grills, slowly dispersing smoke throughout the cooking process. Cast iron ones, although the most costly, are the most successful at maintaining heat and are the easiest to "top off" as the chips burn out. To make a foil smoker pouch for a gas grill, place soaked wood chips in the center of a heavy-duty sheet of foil. Fold the edges together to make a tight seal and flatten the package like an envelope. Using the end of a knife, poke several holes in the top of the package to allow the smoke to escape. Place the pouch directly over the burners, under the grill bars. Heat the grill to hot until smoke appears, then adjust to the desired temperature. For charcoal grills, use a grill box or simply scatter soaked chips over the coals.

Heavy-duty oven mitts

Particularly useful when you are dealing with grill pans on the grill or drip pans, which may need to be moved around while still very hot.

GRILLING INFO

Make sure you have a level site for your grill, away from any overhanging trees, and never leave a lit grill unattended. Heat the grill in advance and rub the grill with a little oil before cooking. Gas grills generally take about 10 minutes to get up to temperature, whereas charcoal grills take about 30 minutes to reach the required temperature and for the smoke to die down. Indoor grill pans take about 5 minutes to come up to temperature. See "Getting the temperature right," page 18, to ensure that you are cooking over the correct temperature. Choosing the right grill is a very personal choice. Make sure you shop around and find the best deal. Here are a few pointers which may make your decision a little easier, but ultimately your choice will be dictated by the space you have available and the taste you are after:

Gas grills

These are usually the choice of the city dweller who can't be bothered dealing with the mess of charcoal and just wants to light the grill at the flick of a switch. The advantage of gas grills is that they almost always come with a fold-down lid, which means the grill can work like a conventional oven as well as a traditional grill. This is useful for cooking more stubborn joints such as chicken drumsticks and whole legs of lamb. A gas grill also gives you more control over temperature than a charcoal one. Choose one with both a grill plate and a hot plate so you can cook several meats and vegetables at the same time. Cleaning is also quick and easy in comparison to charcoal models.

Charcoal grills

Some people just love getting their hands dirty, and the sight of real flames cooking their food with the smell of charcoal is enough to keep them from converting to gas. There are several types of charcoal grills available on the market. The first, and cheapest, is the disposable grill. These are readily available in supermarkets and are suitable for one-time uses like picnics and camping. They consist of a foil container filled with charcoal and topped with a fuel-soaked pad and mesh wiring. They are easy to light and are usually ready to cook on in about 20 minutes. It is important to keep your food moving, as heat cannot be controlled. This applies also to the simple fire box or stand barbecues. Occasionally they will have the added advantage of a moveable grilling rack to lower the food if liked. These barbecues usually have the disadvantage of no air vents for controlling heat.

The kettle barbecue is more advanced and usually comes with controllable air vents, moveable racks and a lid. It acts in the same fashion as a conventional oven. Kettle barbecues are usually made of steel, with a porcelain-enamelled coating which will stand up to numerous barbecue sessions.

It is worth learning how to tell when your charcoal is ready to cook on. A charcoal grill takes about 30 minutes before it is ready but, there can be variations. The coals should be covered with a light grey ash, with a bare glimmer of red glow underneath. Do not start cooking until the flames have died down or you will end up with charred food that is still raw in the center.

Grill pans

These are invaluable for year-round indoor grilling and many models also transfer happily to the grill rack and oven. Their versatility makes them an essential item in any kitchen. The best grill pans are made of cast iron. If cooking indoors, they are much easier to handle over gas elements, which makes for greater control over temperature. Never oil your grill pan while hot but instead lightly oil the food if necessary. Get the exhaust fans going and heat your dry pan to very hot before you add the food. To test if the pan is hot enough, splash over a little water; it should evaporate immediately. Sear the food quickly then reduce the heat to the desired cooking temperature

(see "Getting the temperature right," page 18). Try not to over-crowd your pan or the heat will dramatically decrease.

CLEANING

Clean your grill rack using a wire brush and warm soapy water or crumpled foil at the end of long tongs in preparation for your next barbecue.

For a gas grill, burn off food by keeping the grill on for an extra 10 minutes and scraping off any burnt-on residue using a wire brush, crumpled foil or a metal scraper.

If you are cooking on a charcoal grill, take time to empty and clean out the firebox after each use. Always allow the charcoal to go cold naturally rather than immersing it in water, which may damage the base of the grill. Cover the grill with a lid (if you have one) and close any air vents. Leave overnight and the embers will eventually die. Store away from the damp, dirt and cobwebs when not in use and disconnect the gas if using a gas grill.

Indoor grill pans should never be immediately immersed in cold water as the cast iron might fracture. Allow the pan to cool first, loosen any charred food deposits and wash in plenty of hot soapy water. Always dry your grill pan thoroughly and lightly oil before storing it until the next use.

Getting the temperature right

In all of our recipes we have used consistent terminology in order to help you get the cooking times right. Depending on whether you are cooking over a gas grill, a charcoal grill or on an indoor grill pan, the basic principles are the same. You will need to use your own initiative sometimes as every piece of equipment varies. If your grill has a moveable rack, it is much easier and quicker to adjust the temperature. Likewise, if you are cooking indoors over gas elements rather than electric elements, the temperature can be more quickly adjusted. Light or heat your cooking apparatus according to the manufacturer's directions, then adjust it to the right temperature.

Hold your hand over the grill bar, hot plate or grill pan to test the temperature:

Low – you should be able to keep your hand there indefinitely but still feel warmth. This temperature is useful for holding cooked meat when you are not ready to serve.

Medium – you should be able to hold your hand there for 6–7 seconds. This temperature "cooks" the meat and is generally used for larger cuts and longer cooking recipes.

Medium-hot – you should be able to hold your hand there for 3–4 seconds. This temperature will "sizzle" the food.

Hot – you should be able to hold your hand there for 1 second only. This temperature is useful for food wrapped in banana leaves or foil.

Very hot – this is useful for searing meats such as steak and tuna when a rare center is desired and very quick cooking applies. Don't hold your hand over at this temperature; it's far too hot.

Handy hints for meat and fish

CHICKEN AND DUCK

To butterfly a chicken

Place the bird breast-side down on a flat surface. Cut down both sides of the backbone, using poultry shears or sharp kitchen scissors. Discard the backbone and snip about ½in (1cm) through the wishbone into the breastbone, turn the bird over and press it down flat. To secure the bird in this flattened position it is sometimes helpful to insert two long metal skewers through the bird. Push one skewer horizontally through the wings and breasts and the other horizontally through the thighs. This also makes it easier to handle and turn the bird while cooking. It is best to start cooking a butterflied chicken bone-side down, as the heat will take longer to penetrate through the dense bones. You can butterfly your chicken a day in advance and leave it prepared and covered in the fridge. The same procedure applies for quail, pheasant, poussin and any other bird.

To butterfly a chicken breast

Place the chicken breast on a flat surface. Hold the breast with one hand and, using a sharp knife, slice through the middle horizontally to cut it almost in half. Open the breast and lay out flat or use as a cavity to stuff the chicken breast. If stuffing the chicken breasts, secure the opening using several large toothpicks or by wrapping the breast in prosciutto, vine leaves or foil. You can prepare your chicken breasts a day in advance and refrigerate, covered, until needed.

To prepare chicken wings

Cut the wing tips off through the joint, using poultry shears or sharp kitchen scissors. You can prepare the wings in advance and refrigerate until needed.

To speed up the cooking of drumsticks

Always make deep slashes through to the bone, on both sides of the drumstick, using poultry shears, sharp kitchen scissors or a sharp knife. This will ensure even cooking without burning.

To check if chicken is cooked through

Insert a small sharp knife into the thickest part of flesh, right down to the bone. The juices should run clear and not pink. If any juices are pink, then continue cooking the chicken a little longer until only clear juices run when a knife is inserted.

To score a duck breast
Hold the breast firmly on a flat surface and, using a sharp knife, cut diagonal slashes, about ¾in (2cm) apart, through the skin to make a diamond pattern. Ensure that you do not cut right through the skin to the flesh or you will lose all the succulent juices during cooking and the skin will not achieve the desired crispiness.

RED MEAT AND PORK
To butterfly a leg of lamb
Put the lamb on a flat surface, skin-side down, and at the wide end of the leg cut around the exposed bone using a sharp, small knife. Cut a slit along the length of the bone to expose it and, using short, shallow cuts and scrapes, ease the bone away from the meat, trying to lose as little meat as possible. Remove the bone and discard. Hold the meat securely on a flat surface and, with the knife, make a lengthways slit through the two thicker parts of the meat, either side of where the bone was, and open out flat. The butterflied lamb can now be cooked flat or stuffed and

rolled. Always secure your stuffed or rolled lamb using kitchen twine or long metal skewers. Alternatively, ask your butcher to do this for you.

To cook the perfect steak
Heat your grill pan or grill to very hot. Lightly brush your steak with a little oil to keep it from sticking. Cook your steak, pressing down slightly with a fish slice to ensure that the whole surface comes in contact with the pan and only turn your steak once! Always rest your steak for a couple of minutes before serving.

To cook steak to your desired doneness
For an 8-oz (225-g) steak, cook for 1½ minutes on each side for a rare and very pink steak. It should be rare but warm all the way through. For medium-rare, cook for 2½–3 minutes on each side. For medium to well done cook for 3–5 minutes on each side or until cooked through.

To cook sausages
Remember these three golden rules:
– Cook sausages slowly to ensure that the skin doesn't burst.
– Never prick a good-quality sausage, as the casing helps to retain moisture.

– Cut the links between the sausages cleanly with a sharp knife. When cooked, a sausage should be cooked right through but still juicy and succulent and not charred.

To prevent sausages from burning on the grill

Pre-cook or poach the sausages in water before barbecuing. To pre-cook sausages put them in barely simmering water and poach for 20–30 minutes. Be careful not to cook them too fast or the skins will burst. Grill a pre-cooked sausage for 5–10 minutes over medium-hot heat. This will heat the sausages through giving them color and a smoky flavor.

FISH AND SHELLFISH

To de-sand shellfish

Put the shellfish in a large bowl or bucket of seawater. Add a large handful of oats or flour and leave overnight. The sand will be sitting in the bottom in the morning. Always leave the bucket in a cool place, preferably outside.

To remove bones from salmon

Use sterilized tweezers or pin-nosed pliers. The bones running in a line just off the center of the spine are called pin bones. For a boneless fillet, pull the bones out at the same angle at which they lie.

To open shellfish without cooking or shucking

Simply put them in the freezer in a single layer for about 1 hour. They will pop open and you will easily be able to remove the top shell.

To deal with a live crayfish

Choose one of the following methods. Plunge the crayfish in boiling water for about 2 minutes. Be careful, as it will try to kick and water may splash. Alternatively, place the crayfish in cold fresh water and it will eventually drown. If you have a sharp knife and a strong arm, hold the crayfish securely on a flat surface and cut between the eyes – the crayfish will die immediately. Finally, you could place the crayfish in the freezer until it no longer moves.

To cut a crayfish in half

Place it belly-side down and insert a large knife into the cross mark right behind the head, then cut through the head. Turn the crayfish around and, holding it firmly, cut it in half right through the head to the tail.

To test if fish is cooked

Press the fish using your finger or a fork. The fish should "give" and just start to flake apart in the center.

Starters

Starters are small, decadent offerings to titillate the palate. Decadence and cost, however, usually go hand in hand. But that's the beauty of the starter; its size warrants affordability, while its ingredients guarantee delight. This explains why Pippa and I have been known to order two starters at a restaurant and bypass the main altogether. This isn't a calorie-saving endeavor, simply a craving for a little bit of decadence.

Starters are also considered appeasement food. When my friend Colin lights up his grill, he likes to cook up a quick stir-fry over the grills for the guests to enjoy while he works on the main event. Sometimes it will be scallops and broccoli tossed with sesame and garlic, other times prawns with sweet chillies and lime smoked over a handful of apple wood chips. These dishes tide things over, he says, they take the edge off guests' hunger and keep everyone happy. Appease away, my friend.

Eggplant mash with pork chipolatas

Smoky

This is a modern take on sausage and mash, and the advantage is that it can all be cooked on the grill or in the same grill pan – saving on dishes.

Serves 4

2–3 large eggplants, about 2lb 4oz (1kg) in total, halved
2–3 Tbsp olive oil
2 cloves garlic, crushed
2 tsp sumac or juice of 1 lemon
1 small handful parsley, chopped
Scant ½ cup (100ml) crème fraîche or sour cream
Salt and freshly ground black pepper
12 pork chipolatas, about 1lb (450g) in total,
  or 24–30 small chipolatas or other pork sausages
2 tsp chopped parsley, to serve

Brush the cut surface of the eggplants with oil and grill them over low to medium heat for about 20–30 minutes, turning frequently, until soft, mushy and brown, but still holding their shape. Remove the eggplants and cool slightly. Mash the eggplant flesh using a fork. Add the garlic, sumac, parsley, crème fraîche, salt and pepper and mash further until combined. Set aside while you cook the sausages.

Preheat the grill or grill pan to medium and cook the sausages for 6–8 minutes, turning frequently, until golden brown and cooked through. Serve the eggplant mash in a bowl, topped with chopped parsley, with the sausages on the side.

■ *A green salad and Mediterranean Flatbread (see page 171) can be served with this dish to make a light meal.*

Eggplant mash with pork chipolatas

Peaches wrapped in prosciutto

Juicy

To paraphrase a friend, "a grilled peach wrapped in prosciutto is truly one of those things in this world that is only fully defined by the word 'miracle.'"

Makes 16 individual
  skewers

2 **peaches**
8 pieces **very thinly sliced
  prosciutto**
16 **small, cocktail sized
  skewers,** soaked for 30
  minutes if wooden
Olive oil, for brushing

Preheat grill or grill pan to medium heat.

Cut peaches in half, remove stones, then cut each half into fours. Place prosciutto on a chopping board and slice each piece in half lengthwise. Wrap the peach wedges with prosciutto and place one on the end of each skewer.

Brush each wrapped peach with oil and grill for 2–3 minutes per side, until the prosciutto is crispy and the peaches are slightly charred. Remove from the grill and serve immediately.

Peaches wrapped in prosciutto

Chicken wings – four ways
Sticky

These are finger-licking good and a hit with both young and old!

Makes 20

For the soy, honey and sesame marinade:
20 large chicken wings
2 cloves garlic, crushed
⅔ cup (150ml) soy sauce
Scant ½ cup (100ml) runny honey
Juice of 1 lemon
1 Tbsp sesame seeds

For the chilli marinade:
20 large chicken wings
Scant 1 cup (200ml) cider vinegar
2 Tbsp vegetable oil
2 Tbsp Worcestershire sauce
2 Tbsp tabasco sauce
8 Tbsp tomato ketchup
2 tsp chilli powder
2 Tbsp extra-fine sugar

For the sweet and sour marinade:
20 large chicken wings
Scant ½ cup (100ml) tomato ketchup
Scant ½ cup (100ml) cider vinegar
½ cup (100g) extra-fine sugar
Scant ½ cup (100ml) water
2 cloves garlic, crushed

For the maple syrup and mustard marinade:
20 large chicken wings
Scant ½ cup (100ml) maple syrup
2 tsp Dijon mustard
2 Tbsp Worcestershire sauce
2 Tbsp vegetable oil
2 tsp dried oregano
Juice of 1 lemon

Cut the tips from the wings, through the joint, using poultry shears or sharp kitchen scissors. Put the chicken wings in a large plastic bag or non-metallic bowl and set aside.

Put your chosen marinade ingredients in a small saucepan and bring to a boil. Reduce the heat and simmer for 5 minutes. Cool for 5 minutes, pour over the chicken wings and allow to marinate for 30 minutes. Alternatively, do not cook the marinade first but combine the ingredients and pour cold over the chicken wings, then leave to marinate for at least 2 hours or overnight in the refrigerator, turning occasionally.

Preheat the grill to medium-hot and cook the chicken wings for 20–25 minutes, turning frequently until cooked through and no pink juices are released when a skewer is inserted into the center. Alternatively, cook in an oven preheated to 400°F/200°C for about 25 minutes, or until cooked. Serve hot, warm or cold with lots of paper napkins and finger dipping bowls.

■ *These are delicious served cold and make a great addition to kids' school lunches or picnics.*

Soy-ginger chicken in banana leaf

Fragrant

Try making these using salmon cubes instead of chicken. Just reduce the cooking time to 6–7 minutes. The banana leaf imparts a delicious, fragrant flavor.

Makes about 24

¼ cup (50ml) **light soy sauce**
¼ cup (50ml) **rice wine**
1 Tbsp **grated fresh ginger**
2 Tbsp **soft dark brown sugar**
4 **chicken breasts**
2 **banana leaves**

Place the soy sauce, rice wine, ginger and sugar in a saucepan and bring to a boil. Reduce the heat and simmer for about 5 minutes or until just slightly thickened. Leave to cool.

Cut the chicken into cubes, about 1in (2.5cm) square and put in a shallow dish. Pour the cooled soy mixture over the chicken and leave to marinate for at least 20 minutes or up to 4 hours in the refrigerator, turning once or twice.

Just before you are ready to start cooking, wash the banana leaves and use a sharp knife to remove the thick central rib. Cut the leaves into rectangles large enough to enclose one of the cubes of chicken. To prevent the banana leaf from splitting when folded, pass it over a gas flame or put it under an electric grill until it becomes pliable. Put a cube of chicken on each rectangle of banana leaf and fold the leaf over to enclose the chicken completely. Secure the parcel with a wooden cocktail stick. When the parcels are all made, cook them over a hot grill for about 8–10 minutes or until the chicken is cooked, turning once or twice during cooking. Serve immediately.

Unwrap the parcels before eating and use the cocktail sticks to pick up the chicken.

Soy-ginger chicken in banana leaf

Tomato and goat's cheese bruschettas

Fragrant

These quick and simple bruschettas can be served with any number of different toppings. Try broad beans, when they're in season, with pecorino cheese and mint. Grilled sardines are another favorite.

Serves 4

8 slices **day-old ciabatta,** cut into slices about ½in (1cm) thick
2 **cloves garlic,** peeled
Extra virgin olive oil
8 **bunches red or yellow cherry tomatoes on the vine**
   (about 4–5 **tomatoes per bunch)**
1 **medium bunch oregano**
5oz (150g) **goat's cheese,** crumbled
Sea salt and freshly ground black pepper

Preheat the grill plate or grill pan to medium. Toast the bread slices for about 2 minutes on each side, or until lightly golden and crisp. Remove the bruschettas and rub one side of each slice with the garlic cloves.

Arrange the bruschettas on a serving plate, garlic-side up. Drizzle the tomatoes with a little olive oil and grill for about 3–4 minutes, moving occasionally and keeping them as intact as possible. Transfer the tomatoes to the serving plate and arrange one bunch on each slice of bread. Sprinkle over some oregano leaves and goat's cheese. Drizzle with a little more olive oil and season generously.

Mussel fritters

Textural

A Tribeca and Paroa Bay specialty – thanks to Chris for disclosing your recipe to the world.

Makes 12

1 **egg**
Sea salt and freshly
   ground black pepper
4–5 Tbsp **self-rising flour**
generous ¼ cup–scant
   ½ cup (75–100ml) **beer**
2lb 4oz (1kg) **mussels**
   or clams, steamed open
   and shells discarded,
   meat roughly chopped
1 **onion,** finely chopped
1 **handful cilantro,**
   chopped
Olive oil, for cooking

To serve:
Lemon wedges
Sweet Thai chilli sauce
   (see page 167) or
   tomato sauce

Beat the egg, salt and pepper together in a large bowl. Add the flour slowly and, using a whisk, combine to a thick glue-like consistency. Add enough beer, stirring continuously, to make a smooth batter similar in consistency to thick custard. Add the mussels, chopped onion and cilantro and gently stir to combine.

Heat the grill hot plate to medium and brush over a little oil. Spoon on the mixture to form fritters about 4in (10cm) in diameter. Cook the fritters for 3–4 minutes on the first side; turn and cook for a further 2–3 minutes on the other side or until cooked through. Alternatively, make bite-sized fritters and adjust the cooking time accordingly, about 2 minutes each side. Continue until all the mixture has been used up and serve with lemon wedges and Sweet Thai chilli sauce or tomato sauce on the side.

Sardines on sourdough bread
Rustic

The reason sardines are recommended for barbecue cooking is that if cooked indoors, the smell seems to linger for days.

Serves 4–6

12–18 **small sardines,** ungutted
2 Tbsp **lemon juice**
2 Tbsp **extra virgin olive oil** plus extra to serve
Sea salt and freshly ground black pepper
1 tsp **chilli flakes**
1 **clove garlic**

To serve:
1 **round loaf sourdough bread**
Butter
2 **lemons,** cut into wedges
1 small bunch **parsley,** chopped

Make two to three shallow slashes in each side of the sardines and set aside in a shallow dish.

Combine the lemon juice, olive oil, salt, pepper, chilli flakes and garlic and pour over the sardines, making sure they are well covered. Cover and leave the sardines to marinate for at least 30 minutes, or refrigerate and marinate overnight.

Preheat the grill to medium-hot and place the sardines flat in a hinged wire rack. You may need to do two batches. Grill the sardines over the coals for 3–4 minutes on each side or until opaque throughout and crispy on the outside. If you don't have a hinged rack, or are not cooking over coals, cook on the rack part of your grill instead.

Just before serving, slice the bread thinly and butter it. Put one or two slices of buttered bread and a couple of lemon wedges on each plate. Put the sardines on the bread and drizzle with a little olive oil. Sprinkle with parsley and serve immediately.

Sardines on sourdough bread

Jumbo shrimp with chilli and cilantro

Succulent

These are a great way to start a meal. Just make sure you have plenty of paper towels handy and some water for dipping sticky fingers.

Serves 4–6

24 **raw jumbo shrimp,** peeled and deveined
Juice of 1 **lime**
2 Tbsp **olive oil**
1 Tbsp **fish sauce**
1 bunch **cilantro,** finely chopped
1 **red chilli,** deseeded and finely chopped
2 **cloves garlic,** crushed
Freshly ground black pepper
Lime wedges, to serve

Rinse the shrimp and pat dry with paper towels. Set aside in a non-metallic bowl while you prepare the marinade. Combine the lime juice, olive oil, fish sauce, cilantro, chilli, garlic and black pepper in a small bowl. Mix to combine and pour over the prawns. Stir gently to combine, cover, and refrigerate for at least 1 hour or up to 6 hours.

Preheat the grill hot plate or grill pan to medium-hot. Cook the shrimp for 2–3 minutes, turning once and pouring over the used marinade halfway through cooking. The flesh should turn pink and opaque. Serve hot, with lime wedges.

■ *Sweet Thai chilli sauce (see page 167) is delicious served on the side for dipping.*

Spicy masala drumsticks

Aromatic

Try using this recipe as a guide and experiment with other yogurt-based marinades. Yogurt and saffron or yogurt and Gran's plum sauce (see page 167) work really well too.

Serves 4–6

12 **chicken drumsticks**
2 **cloves garlic,** crushed
1 tsp **finely grated fresh ginger**
1 tsp **ground cumin**
2 Tbsp **garam masala (see Glossary)**
1 tsp **turmeric**
1 tsp **chilli powder**
1 tsp **salt**
Juice of ½ **lemon**
½ **onion,** grated
Scant 1 cup (200g) **plain, unsweetened yogurt**

Slash the drumsticks, using a sharp knife or poultry shears, about two to three times on each side (see page 19). Transfer to a plastic bag or non-metallic bowl and set aside while you make the marinade.

In a bowl combine all the remaining ingredients and mix to combine. Pour the marinade over the chicken and mix well ensuring that the marinade gets into all the slashes. Seal the bag or cover the bowl and leave for at least 1–2 hours or overnight in the refrigerator.

When you are ready to cook, preheat the grill or grill pan to medium. Cook the drumsticks for about 25–35 minutes, or until golden (not burned) and cooked through. No pink juices should run when a knife is inserted into the thickest part of the drumstick. Serve the drumsticks immediately or leave to cool and eat them with your fingers.

Sesame tuna with marinated cucumber

Sesame tuna with marinated cucumber

Tender

For rare tuna, sear it quickly over a hot temperature. For not so rare, use a medium heat and cook for 2–3 minutes each side.

Serves 4–6

1 **tuna fillet, about** 1lb 10oz –2lb 4oz (750g–1kg)
1 Tbsp **sesame oil**
4 Tbsp **black sesame seeds**
4 Tbsp **white sesame seeds**

For the cucumber salad:
1 **cucumber**
Salt and freshly ground black pepper
Juice of 2 **lemons**
2 Tbsp **extra virgin olive oil**

To serve:
Lemon wedges
Wasabi (optional)

Pat the tuna dry and cut into thick batons approximately 2in (5cm) wide and ¾in (2cm) thick. Rub the sesame oil evenly over the tuna batons.

In a large shallow dish or tray, combine the sesame seeds and roll the tuna in the seeds, coating it evenly.

Put the tuna in a clean dish, cover and refrigerate until you are ready to cook.

To prepare the cucumber salad, slice the unpeeled cucumber, using a floating blade vegetable peeler to give you long strips. Work your way around the cucumber but try to avoid too many seeds if you can. Put the cucumber in a bowl with the salt, pepper, lemon juice and olive oil. Mix well and leave to marinate for at least 30 minutes.

Preheat the grill hot plate or grill pan to hot and sear the tuna batons on each side for about 30 seconds to 1 minute, then remove from the pan and allow to rest for 5 minutes. Cut the tuna into ½-in (1-cm) thick slices and serve with the cucumber salad, lemon wedges and wasabi on the side.

Mediterranean stuffed squid

Tender

Fresh squid are a favorite in the coastal towns of almost all Mediterranean countries.

Serves 4–6

4–6 **large squid about**
   1lb 2oz (500g) in total
1¾ cups (150g) **fresh
   breadcrumbs**
1 **chilli,** deseeded and finely
   chopped
1 handful **oregano,**
   chopped
1 handful **parsley,** chopped
Grated rind of 1 **lemon**
1 **clove garlic,** crushed
2 Tbsp **olive oil plus extra
   for cooking**
½ tsp **salt**
**Salt and freshly ground
   black pepper**
Lemons cut into wedges,
   to serve

Wash the squid and pull the tentacles out from the body. Discard the transparent quill if it is still there and rinse the inside of the squid. Pat dry using paper towel.

Put the breadcrumbs, chilli, herbs, lemon rind, garlic, 2 Tbsp oil and ½ tsp salt in a food processor and process for about 1 minute, or until the mixture comes together slightly but is still coarse. Loosely pack the stuffing into the squid bodies, ensuring that you do not stuff them completely full. Secure the ends using cocktail sticks. When all the squid are stuffed, drizzle over a little extra oil and season with salt and pepper.

Preheat the grill or grill pan to medium-hot and cook the squid for about 2–3 minutes on each side, or until the flesh sets white and is firm. Slice the squid into about 4–5 pieces and serve hot with lemon wedges on the side.

Mediterranean stuffed squid

Main meals

A food's taste is shaped by how we react to its texture, smell, temperature, color and degree of spiciness. According to Diane Ackerman in *A Natural History of the Senses*, sound also plays an important role: "There's a satisfying crunch to a fresh carrot stick, a seductive sizzle to a steak, a rumbling frenzy to soup coming to a boil..." Finally, someone to validate the importance of our grilling soundtrack.

Cold-day barbecues call for warm music. This is when Cuba's *Buena Vista Social Club* comes on. Cajun foods, such as Blackened halibut (page 69) go hand in hand with New Orleans Funk and Soul. A little Saturday Night Fish Fry, featuring the fine Irma Thomas singing *Don't Mess with My Man* fits the bill. Auckland barbecues require tunes from the homeland. Crowded House or Split Enz will sweeten the warm air and barbecue aromas.

Always treat the main event seriously by properly awakening the senses. Light the grill, turn on the tunes and travel with sound and flavor.

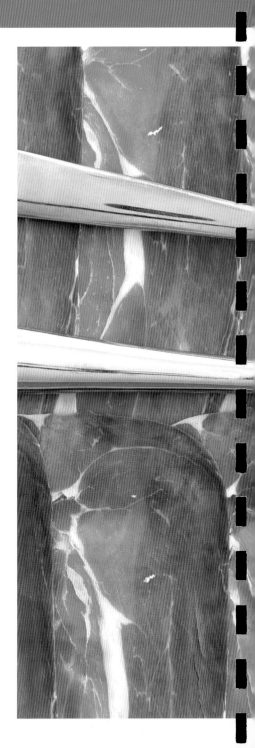

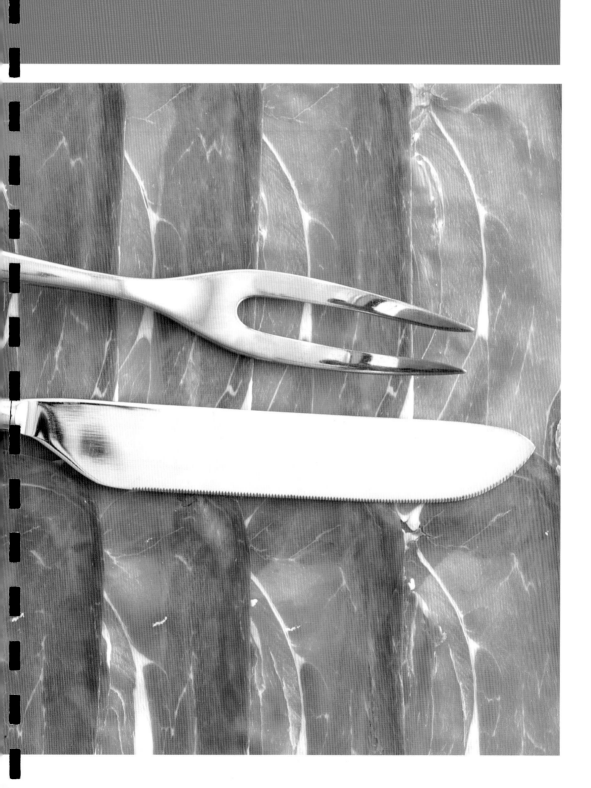

Teriyaki pork tenderloin

Impressive

This is the perfect, quick, stand-by recipe that will never fail to impress. It is served with a spicy vermicelli salad.

Serves 4

1lb 2oz (500g) **pork tenderloin**
½ tsp **sesame oil**
3 Tbsp **light soy sauce**
3 Tbsp **mirin or rice wine**
1½ Tbsp **sweet soy sauce**
2 **cloves garlic**, crushed
1 tsp **grated fresh ginger**

For the vermicelli salad:
1–2 **bird's eye chillies**, finely chopped
2 **spring onions**, sliced
1 small handful **cilantro**, chopped
1–2 Tbsp **brown sugar**
2 Tbsp **fish sauce**
Juice of 2 **limes**
7oz (200g) **vermicelli noodles**, cooked

Trim any sinew from the pork and set the meat aside in a dish. In a small bowl combine the sesame oil, light soy sauce, mirin, sweet soy sauce, garlic and ginger.

Pour the marinade over the pork and turn to coat evenly. Cover and leave the pork to marinate for at least 30 minutes or up to 24 hours in the refrigerator.

When you are ready to cook, heat the grill or grill pan to hot. Add the pork and cook for 3–4 minutes, then turn it and reduce the heat to medium. Continue cooking, turning several times, for a further 10–12 minutes or until the pork is cooked and only clear juices run when it is cut. Remove from the heat, cover and leave to rest for 5 minutes.

Combine all the ingredients for the salad, except the noodles, in a small bowl. Mix to combine then pour the dressing over the cooked noodles. Chill until you are ready to serve. Serve the pork, sliced, with the spicy noodle salad on the side.

Fillet of beef with horseradish cream

Simplicity

The beef fillet tenderloin should always be cooked quickly and, in my opinion, never served well done.

Serves 6–8

For the horseradish cream:
⅔ cup (150g) **plain yogurt**
¼ cup (50g) **horseradish**
Scant ¾ cup (75g) **chopped walnuts**
Freshly ground black pepper

1 x 4lb 8-oz (2-kg) **fillet of beef (tenderloin)**
2 Tbsp **extra virgin olive oil**
2 **cloves garlic,** crushed
Freshly ground black pepper

Combine the yogurt, horseradish, walnuts and black pepper in a bowl. Refrigerate until ready to serve.

When you are ready to cook the beef, preheat the grill to medium-hot. Prepare the beef by trimming any fat from it and slicing off the silver skin. Fold the thin end under so the tenderloin is the same thickness at both ends and secure with kitchen string. Rub over the oil and garlic and season generously with black pepper. Sear the beef on each of its four sides for 3–4 minutes or until golden. If you have a grill with different grilling levels, raise the beef towards the top, reduce the heat slightly and pull down the lid. If you cannot move the beef, then reduce the heat to low and cover with foil or an upside-down roasting dish. Cook the beef for a further 20–25 minutes. Remove the meat and leave to rest, covered, for a further 5–10 minutes before slicing. Slice the meat thinly and serve with horseradish cream on the side.

Butterflied leg of lamb with salsa verde

Herbaceous

Whenever I am back in New Zealand, lamb is always my first request, but it has to be cooked outdoors on the grill!

Serves 4–6

4lb 8-oz (2-kg) **leg of lamb, boned and butterflied** (see page 20)

For the salsa verde:
¾ cup (45g) **flat-leaf parsley**
¼ cup (5g) **mint**
¼ cup (5g) **basil**
1oz (25g) **anchovy fillets**
1 **clove garlic,** chopped
1 Tbsp **capers**
Scant ½ cup (100ml) **extra virgin olive oil**
Sea salt and freshly ground black pepper

Hold the leg of lamb firmly with the flat of your hand. Using a sharp knife, slice the thickest part of the meat, keeping the knife horizontal, to open up a flap which can be stuffed. Set aside.

Combine all the salsa verde ingredients in a food processor and blend to a paste. The mixture will be quite wet. Spread the salsa verde in between the meat flaps and secure using three metal skewers. Rub any extra salsa verde over the outside of the lamb. Leave the meat to marinate in the fridge for at least 30 minutes or up to 24 hours.

Remove the lamb from the fridge 20 minutes before cooking. Preheat the grill to medium-hot. Cook the lamb for 15 minutes on each side for medium-rare or 20 minutes on each side for well done. If cooking indoors, preheat the oven to 400°F/200°C and the grill pan to medium-hot. Cook the lamb for 4–5 minutes on each side in the grill pan or until golden brown. Cover with foil and transfer to the oven for a further 20 minutes for medium-rare, or 25 minutes for well done.

Venison steaks with juniper rub

Spiced

If you're not a fan of polenta, try serving these steaks with a large bowl of new potatoes or mashed potatoes.

Serves 4

4 **venison steaks** about 5oz (150g) **each**
8–12 **juniper berries**
2 tsp **sea salt**
1 tsp **black peppercorns**
2 tsp **coriander seeds**
1lb 2oz (500g) **cooked, shaped polenta,** home-made or store-bought
1 Tbsp **olive oil**
Gran's plum sauce (see page 167), to serve

Pat the venison steaks dry and set aside on a flat plate. Put the juniper berries, salt, peppercorns and coriander seeds in a spice grinder and grind for 2–3 minutes to a fine-to-coarse powder. Alternatively, grind by hand using a pestle and mortar. Rub the spice mix over both sides of the venison steaks and refrigerate for at least 30 minutes or until you are ready to cook.

Just before cooking the steaks, preheat the grill or grill pan to medium-hot. Slice the polenta into ½-in (1-cm) thick pieces, brush with a little oil and cook for about 3 minutes on each side, or until golden, crisp and warmed through. Cook the steaks for about 2 minutes on each side, depending on thickness, or until golden and cooked through but still slightly rare if liked.

Put about three slices of polenta on each plate, top with a venison steak and serve with Gran's plum sauce on the side.

Five-spice roasted and grilled pork belly

Crispy

This recipe is a little time-consuming. You can roast the pork in advance so there is not too much to do on the day.

Serves 4–6

2 Tbsp **Chinese 5-spice powder (see Glossary)**
2 tsp **grated fresh ginger**
2 **cloves garlic,** crushed
2 Tbsp **fish sauce**
1 Tbsp **lemon juice**
¾ cup (100g) **brown sugar**
14-oz (400-g) **can chopped tomatoes**
2 Tbsp **tomato paste**
3lb 5-oz (1.5–2-kg) **piece pork belly,** bones removed, rind on and slashed
Gran's plum sauce (see page 167) and grilled cherry tomatoes, to serve

To make the marinade, put all the ingredients (except the pork, plum sauce and cherry tomatoes) in a food processor and purée until smooth. Pour it all over and under the pork, ensuring that you spread it into the slashes. Cover, refrigerate and leave the meat to marinate for 1–2 hours. Preheat the oven to 350°F/180°C. Line a roasting tray with foil and in the center set a rack that is large enough to hold the pork. Place the pork, rind-side down, on the rack and cook towards the top of the oven for 30 minutes. After 30 minutes, baste the pork all over with more marinade. Cook for a further 45 minutes–1 hour, basting every 20 minutes. Turn the meat rind side up, baste and cook for a further 30 minutes. Remove from the oven and allow to cool.

Once cool, slice the pork into ¼–½-in (½–1-cm) slices. Cook on a hot grill or grill pan for 1–2 minutes on each side or until crispy and charred. The fat may spit so be careful. Serve hot, with Gran's Plum Sauce and grilled cherry tomatoes.

Five-spice roasted and grilled pork belly

Butterflied Thai coconut chicken breasts

Fragrant

These chicken breasts become so tender that they almost melt in your mouth. I like to serve them chopped, as part of a chicken salad.

Serves 4

2 Tbsp Sweet Thai chilli sauce (see page 167)
Grated rind and juice of 1 lime
1 Tbsp fish sauce
2 tsp grated fresh ginger
½ cup (10g) cilantro, roughly chopped
⅔ cup (150ml) coconut milk
4 chicken breasts, butterflied (see page 19)

Combine all the ingredients, except the chicken breasts, in a bowl. Put a third of this marinade in a flat dish, place the butterflied chicken breasts on top and pour over the remaining marinade, ensuring that it covers all the chicken. Leave the chicken to marinate in the refrigerator for at least 2 hours or up to 24 hours.

Preheat the grill or grill pan to medium and cook the chicken for 3–4 minutes on the first side, turn, and cook for a further 2–3 minutes or until cooked through and only clear juices run from the meat. Serve the chicken breasts whole with a side dish of rice and vegetables or chop them into a green salad.

■ *This marinade works equally well on firm fish such as monkfish or turbot.*

Butterflied Thai coconut chicken breasts

Spinach and ricotta-stuffed chicken

Spinach and ricotta-stuffed chicken

Fragrant

These chicken breasts always look impressive with their green speckled center and crispy prosciutto coating.

Serves 4–6

1 Tbsp **olive oil**
1 **onion,** finely chopped
2 **cloves garlic,** finely chopped
Grated rind of 1 **lemon**
3½oz (100g) **vacuum-packed chestnuts,** crumbled
Salt and freshly ground black pepper
5 cups (225g) **spinach leaves**
Scant ½ cup (100g) **ricotta or quark**
4–6 **chicken breasts**
8–12 **slices prosciutto**
Green salad, to serve

Heat the oil in a large frying pan. Add the onion and sauté for 2–3 minutes or until translucent. Add the garlic, lemon rind, chestnuts, salt and pepper and sauté for a further 2–3 minutes or until just starting to brown and the mixture is quite dry. Remove from the heat and cool completely.

Cook the spinach in a large saucepan with boiling water until bright green and wilted. Drain and squeeze out any excess water. Cut the spinach finely and set aside. When the chestnut mixture is cool, add the spinach and ricotta and mix well. Season. Cut a pocket in each chicken breast and fill with one-quarter or one-sixth of the mixture, depending on size. Hold the breasts and wrap two slices of prosciutto tightly around them.

Preheat the grill or grill pan to hot and cook the chicken breasts for 6–8 minutes on each side, reducing the heat to medium after about 2 minutes. Continue until cooked through and no pink juices run from the meat when cut. Allow to rest, covered, for about 5 minutes and serve with a green salad.

Mushroom and pancetta-stuffed chicken

Tuscan

This recipe sums up my favorite Italian flavors.

Serves 4–6

1 cup (100g) **dried porcini or wild mushrooms**
2 Tbsp **extra virgin olive oil**
2 **onions**, finely chopped
1 **red chilli**, deseeded and finely chopped
8oz (250g) **pancetta**, cubed
2 **cloves garlic**, crushed
Freshly ground black pepper
4 **sprigs thyme**
3 Tbsp **Marsala (optional)**
4–6 **chicken breasts**

Soak the mushrooms in warm water for about 15 minutes. Heat the oil in a frying pan to moderate heat and sauté the onion and chilli for 1–2 minutes until the onion is translucent but not browned. Add the pancetta, increase the heat and sauté for a further 3–4 minutes until golden, adding the garlic for the last minute. Reduce the heat and season with black pepper. Drain the mushrooms and chop finely. Add the mushrooms and thyme to the pan and sauté for a further 3–4 minutes. If using Marsala, increase the heat for the last 2 minutes and add to the pan, stirring until the liquid has evaporated. Allow the mixture to cool.

Cut a pocket in each chicken breast, ensuring that you do not cut right through. Stuff with the mushroom mixture and secure the cut with a cocktail stick. Refrigerate until you are ready to cook, up to 6 hours.

Preheat the grill or grill pan to hot and cook the breasts for 6–8 minutes on each side, depending on size, reducing the heat to medium after about 2 minutes. Continue until the chicken is cooked through and no pink juices run from the meat when cut. Allow to rest, covered, for about 5 minutes.

Whole chilli snapper in banana leaf

Interactive

This is my favorite kind of barbecue food – its interactive nature means that everyone just dives in!

Serves 4

2 **snapper, about** 1lb 10oz (750g) **each,** gutted and scaled
⅔ cup (150ml) **Sweet Thai chilli sauce (see page 167) or store-bought**
2 **whole banana leaves**
2 **lemons,** sliced
2 **handfuls cilantro**
2 **lemons,** cut into wedges

Using a sharp knife cut shallow, diagonal, parallel slashes ¾in (2cm) apart through the snapper skin to make diamond shapes. Put the fish on two separate deep-sided plates and pour half of the Sweet Thai chilli sauce over each. Rub the sauce into the slashes and cavity of the fish. Cover the plates with plastic wrap and leave in the fridge for 30 minutes or up to 6 hours.

Preheat the grill to medium-hot and have a grill rack positioned. Trim the hard edge from both of the banana leaves and wash well under cold water. Pass over a gas flame or put under an electric grill until it becomes pliable. Put about 6–8 lemon slices and a handful of cilantro into the cavity of each fish. Put the fish on the banana leaf. Pour over a little of the sauce that has run off. Pull the side of the leaf up and over the fish, making a parcel, and secure with bamboo skewers.

Lightly oil the banana leaf and place the parcel of fish on the grill. Cook for about 20–25 minutes, opening up the parcel for the last 3–5 minutes. The fish is ready if it flakes when a skewer is inserted. Serve straight from the banana leaf parcels with roughly torn cilantro scattered on top and lemon wedges on the side.

Five-spice duck breasts
Easy

It is essential to score the duck correctly in order to get a crispy skin and juicy flesh (see page 20). If you cut too far in you, will risk losing all the nice juices and the skin won't crisp up.

Serves 4

4 **duck breasts**, skin on
2 tsp **Chinese 5-spice powder (see Glossary)**
4 heads **bok choy**
1 tsp **olive oil**

Pat the duck breasts dry using paper towel. With a sharp knife, cut diagonal, parallel slashes ¾in (2cm) apart through the skin to make diamond shapes. Make sure that you do not cut right through and pierce the flesh. Rub ½ tsp of the Chinese 5-spice powder into the skin and flesh of the breast. Repeat with the remaining duck breasts. These can be left in the fridge for up to 12 hours.

To prepare the bok choy, bring a saucepan of water to the boil and plunge the bok choy in for about 1 minute, or until bright green in color. Remove the heads immediately and cool under running cold water. Halve the bok choy lengthways and set aside.

Preheat the grill or grill pan to medium-hot. Cook the duck skin-side down for about 5–6 minutes, until the skin is crispy. Turn and cook for a further 8–10 minutes, depending on how well done you like your duck. Remove from the grill or grill pan, cover with foil and allow to rest for 5 minutes. While the duck rests, cook the bok choy on the grill or grill pan for about 1 minute flat-side down and a further minute on the second side. Slice the duck just before serving and serve with one or two halves of bok choy.

Five-spice duck breasts

Grilled crayfish with lemon butter

Indulgence

To me, grilled crayfish and a glass of chilled New Zealand Sauvignon Blanc is the ultimate satisfaction.

Serves 2–4

For the lemon butter:
1¼ sticks (150g) **butter,** softened
Finely grated rind of 2 **lemons**
Salt and freshly ground black pepper

2 **large crayfish or lobster,** live if possible
1 Tbsp **olive oil**
4 **lemons,** halved
1 **handful basil**

Prepare the lemon butter well in advance. Put the butter, lemon rind, salt and pepper in a food processor and pulse until well blended. Lay out a large piece of foil, about 10in (25cm) square, on a flat surface, put the butter in the center and shape into a log. Roll up the foil, shaping the butter into an even log shape, and twist the ends to secure it.

Refrigerate the butter for at least 4 hours or freeze for about 45 minutes. If cutting the butter while frozen, warm the knife slightly first. Remove the butter from the fridge just before serving to soften slightly.

Kill and cut your crayfish in half (see page 21).

Preheat the grill to medium. Lightly oil the crayfish on the flesh side. Place the crayfish flesh-side down on the hot rack. Grill for 5 minutes. Turn the crayfish over, rub a slice of lemon butter over the surface and cook for 8–10 minutes, moving them around the rack occasionally. For the last 2–3 minutes, place the lemon halves flat-side down on the grill and cook. Serve with grilled lemon halves to squeeze over, another slice of lemon butter and freshly torn basil leaves.

Grilled crayfish with lemon butter

Whisky, garlic and brown sugar salmon

Succulent

My husband's cousin, Gregor Wilson, and his wife Jenny, were married on beautiful Galliano Island in British Columbia. They served wild Pacific salmon, bathed in this marinade, to their guests. The recipe, a long-time family favorite, will elevate any event to celebratory status.

Serves 6

1 **salmon fillet, about** 3lb (1.4kg), skin on
Vegetable oil, for brushing

For the marinade:
½ cup (125ml) **vegetable oil**
2 Tbsp **soy sauce**
2 **cloves garlic,** crushed
2 Tbsp **packed brown sugar**
Generous ¼ cup (75ml) **whisky**

Wipe the salmon and place it in a shallow baking dish. Combine the ingredients for the marinade in a bowl and pour it over the salmon, turning to coat. Leave to marinate in the refrigerator for 1½ hours and then at room temperature for a further 30 minutes.

Preheat the grill or grill pan to very hot and brush with oil. Grill the salmon, skin-side down, for 1 minute then reduce the heat to low. Continue cooking for 2–3 minutes, then carefully turn over and cook for a further 2–3 minutes until cooked through.

■ *Six salmon steaks can be substituted for a fillet.*

Halibut with lemon, basil and garlic

Pure

We are continually trying to replicate that fine summer's evening when my brother-in-law grilled the halibut he had caught in the Pacific. The thick, tender meat and pure, clean flavor was like nothing we had ever tasted – even for fish aficionados like ourselves. I can't guarantee warm evening sun, but I can suggest this marinade – simplicity at its best.

Serves 4

4 **halibut steaks, about** 2lb 4oz (1kg) **in total**
2 **cloves garlic,** thinly sliced
2 Tbsp **basil,** thinly sliced
Juice of 1 **lemon**
½ cup (125ml) **olive oil, plus extra for brushing**
½ tsp **sea salt**
Freshly ground pepper, to taste

Wipe the halibut steaks and place in a shallow baking dish. Whisk the remaining ingredients together in a small bowl. Pour this marinade over the fish, turning to coat. Cover and leave to marinate at room temperature for 30 minutes.

Preheat the grill or grill pan to very hot. Brush the grill rack with oil and place the fish steaks directly on the rack. Cook for 1 minute then reduce the heat to low. Grill for 12–15 minutes, depending on the thickness of the fish, until just cooked through. Carefully lift the steaks from the grill with a long spatula and transfer to serving plates.

Butterflied turkey

Succulent

You will never taste a juicier, more succulent turkey than one straight from a smoky grill. Serve with Cranberry pear chutney on the side (see page 169).

Serves 4–6

1 x 9lb 8-oz (4.5-kg) **turkey**
Scant ½ cup (100ml) **melted butter**
4 **large handfuls apple or cherry wood chips,** soaked for 1 hour

Preheat the grill to medium-hot. Sprinkle a large handful of wet chips over the coals or, if using gas, add soaked chips to a smoke box or place a foil-perforated pack (see page 14) directly on the elements.

Remove the giblets from the cavity of the turkey. Follow instructions for how to butterfly a chicken (see page 62). Lay on a baking tray and brush the top side with melted butter.

Lay the turkey, butter-side down, on the hot grill bars.

Sear for 2 minutes until golden and grill marks appear. Brush the top side with more butter and flip. When both sides are golden and grill marks appear, reduce the heat to medium-low. If using a charcoal grill, transfer the turkey back to a clean baking tray. Push the coals to the side and place a drip pan under the grill bars. Return the turkey to the grill and cover.

Flip it over every 15 minutes and add fresh wood chips every 30 minutes. For a charcoal grill, add 12 unlit pieces of charcoal to each side after 1 hour. Grill for about 2 hours. To check if it is cooked, wiggle a drumstick – it should move freely at the joint.

Allow the turkey to rest for 10 minutes, covered with foil, before carving.

Pepper steak with mustard brandy cream

Fiery

I have always been reluctant to grill pepper steak, fearing that I would lose out on all the pan drippings essential to my accompanying creamy sauce. Until this creation, that is!

Serves 2

1lb 5oz (600g) **sirloin about 1in (2.5cm) thick**
Olive oil, for brushing
2 Tbsp **freshly crushed black peppercorns**
Salt, to taste

For the sauce:
Generous ¼ cup (75ml) **crème fraîche, sour cream or heavy cream**
1 Tbsp **wholegrain Dijon mustard**
1 Tbsp **brandy**
⅛ tsp **salt**

1 **handful watercress,** to garnish
Onions on the grill (see page 149), to serve

Preheat the grill or grill pan to very hot.

Brush the steak(s) with olive oil and pat peppercorns over the top, bottom and sides, pressing gently to coat. Season with salt. Grill the steak(s) for 2 minutes on each side for medium-rare. Transfer to a chopping board and loosely cover with foil.

While the meat rests, whisk the sauce ingredients together (if using heavy cream, whisk vigorously to thicken before you add the remaining ingredients). Spoon the sauce over the steak(s) and garnish with watercress. Serve with Onions on the grill, sliced or whole.

Caramelized lamb chops

Caramelized lamb chops

Spectacular

Grilling meltingly tender, marinated lamb chops is one of life's simple pleasures.

Serves 4

1 cup (20g) **cilantro,** roughly chopped
6 Tbsp **brown sugar**
4 Tbsp **dark soy sauce**
4 Tbsp **mirin, Chinese rice wine or sherry**
4 **cloves garlic,** finely chopped
16 **single-rib lamb chops**

To serve:
Grilled potatoes, green salad or steamed green beans

Combine the cilantro, brown sugar, soy sauce, mirin and garlic in a shallow baking dish. Add the chops, turning well to coat in the marinade. Cover and refrigerate overnight or for up to 24 hours.

Preheat the grill or grill pan to very hot. Brush with oil. Grill the chops to taste (4–6 minutes on each side for medium) until the edges are browned and caramelized. Transfer the chops to a platter and allow to rest for 2–3 minutes before serving with grilled potatoes and a green salad or steamed green beans.

Chef Jon's dry cured salt-sugar salmon

Velvety

Every so often Jon Cox, family friend and incredible chef, breaks free from his Californian kitchen and heads northeast to Nova Scotia. On his last trip he found himself at our family cottage, back in the kitchen, dry-curing salmon for the whole family. His recipe is now a family staple, enjoyed all year around.

Serves 4

Generous ¾ cup (100g) **coarse sea salt**
½ cup (100g) **extra-fine sugar**
Grated rind of 1 lemon
1 Tbsp **fennel seeds (optional)**
4 **salmon fillets, about** 4oz (120g) **each,** skin on
Vegetable oil, for grilling

Combine the salt, sugar, lemon rind and fennel seeds in a shallow baking dish. Bury the fillets in the mixture. Cover with plastic wrap and refrigerate for 2–3 hours.

Remove the fish from the refrigerator 20 minutes before grilling. Heat a grill pan or grill to very hot. Brush the grill with oil. Lift the fillets from the sugar and salt mixture and rinse under running water. The surface of the fish will be deep in color and almost caramelized in texture. Grill, skin-side down, for 4–5 minutes until the skin is charred and the fish is uniform in color. Lift from the grill and serve.

Chef Jon's dry cured salt-sugar salmon

Blackened halibut

Blackened halibut
Crispy heat

A hot grill coupled with a crispy, "blackened" crust adds a fiery, Cajun touch to halibut. New Orleans chef Paul Prudhomme is to thank for putting "blackening" on the culinary map.

Serves 4

For the rub:
1 tsp **salt**
1 tsp **dried thyme**
½ tsp **dried oregano**
½ tsp **cayenne pepper**
¼ tsp **hot paprika**
½ tsp **freshly ground black pepper**
½ tsp **fennel seeds,** toasted and roughly chopped
Salt and pepper, to taste

4 **halibut fillets,** 7oz (200g) each
Olive oil, for brushing
1 **lime,** quartered

Combine the ingredients for the rub in a small bowl. Place the halibut fillets in a shallow baking dish and brush with oil. Pat the rub all over the fish. Season with more salt and pepper. Cover and chill for up to 1 hour, in the refrigerator.

Preheat the grill or grill pan to hot. Brush the grill bars well with oil. Grill the fillets for 2–2½ minutes on each side until charred and just cooked through. Serve immediately with a squeeze of lime.

Pork tenderloin with redcurrant sauce

Savory

This family favorite graces the table on birthdays, holidays and any day in between. Pork tenderloin is as tender as its beef equivalent but is only a fraction of the cost.

Serves 2

1 **pork tenderloin**
Olive oil, for brushing

For the marinade:
1 Tbsp **Dijon mustard**
1 Tbsp **thyme**
1 tsp **dried marjoram**
½ tsp **savory**
½ tsp **salt**
½ tsp **pepper**

For the sauce:
Scant ½ cup (100ml)
   redcurrant or apple jelly
1 Tbsp **Dijon mustard**
1 tsp **red wine vinegar**
Salt and pepper, to taste

Trim the pork of any sinew and place in a shallow dish. Combine the marinade ingredients in a small bowl and rub over the tenderloin. If the ends of the tenderloin taper dramatically, fold them over and secure with kitchen string. Leave to marinate in the fridge for at least 30 minutes. Allow the pork to sit for 20 minutes at room temperature before grilling.

Preheat the grill or grill pan to medium-hot and brush with oil. Place the tenderloin on the grill and grill on all four sides for 3–4 minutes on each side. A meat thermometer, inserted at the thickest point, should read 158°F/70°C. Transfer the meat to a cutting board, loosely cover with foil and leave to rest.

While the meat is grilling, prepare the sauce. Melt the redcurrant or apple jelly in a small saucepan over medium heat. Whisk in the remaining ingredients and simmer gently until it thickens slightly, 3–5 minutes. Slice the pork tenderloin on the diagonal and fan across serving plates. Top with the sauce.

Ribs à l'ancienne

Zesty

Handed down through Acadian families of eastern Canada, this recipe has found its way, happily, into the hands of Jolene d'Entrement. It has won many unofficial neighborhood barbecue cook-offs.

Serves 4

For the sauce:
1 tsp **butter**
4 **cloves garlic,** finely chopped
1 Tbsp **rosemary,** finely chopped
1 cup (250ml) **ketchup**
4 Tbsp **brown sugar**
3 Tbsp **Worcestershire sauce**
3 Tbsp **Dijon mustard**

4 racks **baby back ribs about** 4lb 8oz (2kg)

To make the sauce, melt the butter in a saucepan over medium heat. Add the garlic and rosemary and sauté until fragrant. Add the remaining ingredients and simmer, stirring occasionally, for 10–15 minutes. Set aside.

Cover the bottom of a large pot with water. Fit a steamer inside, cover and bring the water to a boil. Add the ribs, cover and steam for 10–15 minutes until the meat is just cooked through. Remove from the pan and allow to cool slightly. Place the ribs in a large baking dish and cover with half the sauce, turning to coat. Cover with plastic wrap and refrigerate for at least 4 hours.

Preheat the grill to very hot. Cut the rib sections between the bones into individual ribs and arrange on a clean baking sheet. Grill the ribs, brushing well with the remaining sauce, until they are slightly charred and the edges are crispy. Serve warm with any remaining sauce.

Pork ribs with mustard bourbon sauce
Heaven

This recipe takes me back to our little London dinner club, where our good friend Sean was the chef supreme.

Serves 4

For the multi-purpose dry rub:
2 Tbsp **ground cumin**
1 Tbsp **chilli powder**
1 Tbsp **dry mustard powder**
1 Tbsp **coarse sea salt**
1½ tsp **cayenne pepper**
1½ tsp **ground cardamom**
1½ tsp **ground cinnamon**

3lb 5oz (1.5kg) **baby back pork ribs**
Mustard bourbon BBQ sauce (see page 170)

Mix the ingredients for the dry rub in a medium bowl. Rub the mixture over both sides of the rib racks. Arrange the ribs on a large baking sheet. Cover and refrigerate overnight.

Preheat the grill to medium. Cut the rib racks into 4- to 6-rib sections. Arrange the ribs on the grill. Grill until the meat is tender, occasionally turning the ribs with tongs, about 40 minutes. Using tongs, transfer the ribs to a work surface.

Cut the rib sections between the bones into individual ribs. Arrange on a clean baking sheet. Brush the ribs with half of the Mustard bourbon BBQ sauce. Place the remaining sauce in a small saucepan and reserve for use later.

Return the ribs to the grill. Place the pan of reserved sauce at the edge of the grill to reheat. Grill the ribs until brown and crisp on the edges, brushing with more sauce and turning occasionally, about 10 minutes. Serve the ribs with warm sauce.

■ *Try using the multi-purpose dry rub on the Butterflied turkey (see page 62), steaks or chicken.*

Pork ribs with mustard bourbon sauce

Sirloin with chimichurri marinade

Sirloin with chimichurri marinade

Pungent

Chimichurri is a fresh herb-and-vinegar mixture used in Argentinean cuisine both for basting grilled meats and as a condiment. It's incredible with steak, as you will see!

Serves 2

1 cup (250ml) **extra virgin olive oil**
2 Tbsp **chopped thyme**
2 Tbsp **chopped oregano**
2 Tbsp **chopped flat-leaf parsley**
1 Tbsp **chopped rosemary**
1 **chipotle chilli in adobo sauce**, chopped
1 Tbsp **sweet Spanish paprika**
3 **cloves garlic**, finely chopped
3 Tbsp **red wine vinegar**
½ tsp **sea salt**
Freshly ground black pepper
1lb 5oz (600g) **top sirloin steak about** 1in (2.5cm) **thick**

Heat the olive oil in a medium-sized saucepan until hot. Remove from the heat and set aside. Add the remaining ingredients, except for the steak, stir, and leave at room temperature to cool and infuse for 1 hour.

Pour one quarter of this marinade into a dish and add the steak, turning several times to coat. Reserve the remaining marinade to serve with the cooked steak. Cover and refrigerate for 1 hour. Remove and leave at room temperature for 30 minutes.

Preheat the grill or grill pan to very hot and cook the steak for 2 minutes on each side for medium-rare. Transfer the steak to a chopping board and loosely cover with foil. Allow it to rest for 5 minutes before thinly slicing across the grain.

Serve with the reserved marinade.

Steak with sweet and spicy cola sauce

Smoky citrus

Cola, in a sauce? It's a flavorsome liquid characterized by a hint of caramel, a citrus top note and a touch of cinnamon.

Serves 2–3

1 Tbsp **butter**
1 **small onion**, finely chopped
2 **cloves garlic**, crushed
1 Tbsp **finely chopped fresh ginger**
1 **chipotle chilli in adobo sauce**, finely chopped
1¼ cups (300ml) **cola**
Scant 1 cup (200ml) **ketchup**
1 Tbsp **tomato paste**
1 Tbsp **adobo sauce**
Grated rind of 1 **lemon**
2 Tbsp **lemon juice**
1 Tbsp **Dijon mustard**
2 Tbsp **cider vinegar**
1lb 5oz (600g) **flank steak**

Heat the butter in a saucepan over medium heat. Add the onion, garlic, ginger and chilli and sauté over medium heat until the onion becomes translucent. Add the cola and bring to a boil. Whisk in the remaining ingredients (except the steak) and simmer for 25–30 minutes, stirring occasionally, until the sauce thickens. Turn off the heat and allow the sauce to cool.

Place the steak in a shallow baking dish and cover with 1 cup (250ml) sauce, turning to coat. Cover with plastic wrap and refrigerate overnight or for at least 8 hours.

Remove the steak from the refrigerator 30 minutes before cooking. Preheat the grill or grill pan to hot and cook the steak for 2 minutes on each side for medium-rare. Brush the steak with more sauce while grilling. Transfer the steak to a cutting board and loosely cover with foil. Allow it to rest for 5 minutes before thinly slicing across the grain. Serve with the remaining sauce.

Whole chicken on a beer can
Juicy

Grilling chicken on a beer can is a bit of an underground, cult-like operation. This recipe reveals all!

Serves 2–3

1 **can beer**
1 **chicken about** 3lb 5oz (1.5kg)
Olive oil, for brushing
1 **large handful of wood chips – apple or cherry,** soaked for 1 hour

Open the beer can and take a gulp. Make several holes in the top of the can using a can opener. Set aside.

Remove the giblets from the chicken and discard the fat around the neck. Rinse the chicken under cold water, pat dry and brush with oil.

Preheat the grill to medium. If using a charcoal grill, prepare for indirect grilling and place a drip pan in the center among the coals. Sprinkle a large handful of wet chips over the coals, or if using gas, add soaked chips to smoke box or place a foil-perforated pack (see page 15) directly on the elements.

Hold the bird upright, with wings upright and legs dangling below. Lower the chicken on to the beer can, keeping the can upright. If the bird is big enough, the tips of the legs will rest on the grill. Stand the chicken in the center of the grill above the drip pan. Cover. Leave to cook for about 1–1¼ hours, until the skin is dark golden and the thickest part of the bird is 180°F/80°C.

If drippings flare up during cooking, add a little water to the dripping pan. If the bird browns too quickly, gently tent it with foil.

Once cooked, lift the bird off the grill and allow it to rest for 5 minutes. Carve and serve.

Tuna stuffed with sesame greens
Surprising

Ruby-colored, dense, local big-eye tuna fish is the perfect accompaniment to ginger and garlicky sesame greens.

Serves 2

2 **thick tuna steaks about** 7oz (200g) **each and at least** 1¼in (3cm) **thick**
2 **spring onions, white parts only,** finely chopped
1 tsp **finely chopped fresh ginger**
½ tsp **finely chopped garlic**
½ tsp **sesame seeds**
2 tsp **soy sauce**
1 tsp **sesame oil plus extra to baste**
2 tsp **vegetable oil**
Generous ¾ cup (50g) **watercress or other small yet sturdy greens**

Preheat the grill or grill pan to very hot.

Place the tuna steaks on a cutting board. Place one hand firmly on the tuna. With a small, sharp knife, make a small incision into the steak, creating a pocket.

Combine the spring onions, ginger, garlic, sesame seeds, soy sauce, sesame oil and vegetable oil in a small bowl. Toss with the watercress.

Carefully stuff the tossed watercress into each tuna steak, pushing well inside the steaks. Reserve any extra watercress for garnish. Brush the steaks generously with sesame oil and place on the grill. Sear on both sides until browned, about 30 seconds on each side. Reduce the heat (or, if using charcoal, move to an area of the grill where there are no coals underneath) and allow the steaks to cook for 3–4 minutes on each side for medium steaks.

Serve the tuna steaks cut in half to expose the watercress inside. Garnish with any remaining tossed watercress.

Tuna stuffed with sesame greens

Whole trout stuffed with lemon and dill

Whole trout stuffed with lemon and dill

Delicate

My father sometimes brings home fresh trout from his fishing excursions to Nova Scotia's Gibraltar Lake. Cooking whole fish in a foil package steams the fish and allows you to create the buttery, flavorful fillings.

Serves 1

1 **small trout, about** 1lb 2oz (500g), **gutted**
2–3 sprigs **dill**
1 tsp **cold butter,** cut in half
1 **slice lemon,** cut into 4 pieces
Salt and pepper, to taste
Vegetable oil, for brushing

Preheat the grill to medium.

Open the cavity of the fish and place dill, butter and pieces of lemon inside. Season.

Take a sheet of foil one-and-a-half times the length of the fish and brush it lightly with vegetable oil. Place the trout in the center of the foil, bring the long edges together and loosely fold. Scrunch the ends to form a loose yet airtight rectangular package.

Place the package on the grill and cover. Grill for about 8 minutes. To check if the fish is ready, remove the package from the grill, open it and insert a wooden skewer into the thickest part of the fish. If the fish is ready the skewer should glide in easily. If you are unsure, peel back a small piece of skin and look closely at the flesh – if it is still transparent close the package and grill for another 1–2 minutes. When the trout is cooked, unwrap the package and carefully transfer the fish to a plate. Pour butter juices from the package over the fish. Serve.

■ *Substitute any delicate whole fish, such as sea bass or red snapper, for the trout. Ask your fishmonger to gut the fish if you're unsure about doing it yourself.*

Bread in hand

"You're not really serious about barbecuing until you've slept next to your cooker and used a bag of charcoal as a pillow," says "Rockin' Ronnie" Shewchuk, the chief cook of the Canadian champion barbecue team Rockin Ronnie's Butt Shredders. I think you're not serious about grilling until you've had to put on your ski gear, de-ice your grill with a pick axe, shovel off the snow and grill burgers in 5°F (-15°C) weather.

I'm not the only Canadian who will do anything for a burger. We're all like this. We love our barbecues, despite the weather. We grill in horizontal rain, scorching sun, dense fog and snow-storms. When a craving strikes, it must be fulfilled. Admittedly, my barbecue cravings, especially for breads and burgers, are stronger than most. I need to sink my teeth into a thick, juicy patty topped with caramelized onions, mayonnaise and ripe tomatoes. Sometimes it's blue cheese, other times its alfalfa sprouts with peanut sauce. Grilled Portobello mushrooms are easily interchangeable. Chicken breasts are just fine too. My cravings change as often as the weather.

Vegetable and taleggio tortilla toasties
Adaptable

Taleggio is a soft mould-ripened Italian cheese. It is very similar to French soft cheese, so if you can't find it substitute Camembert instead.

Serves 4

1 large eggplant
2 zucchinis
2 red or yellow peppers
2 Tbsp olive oil
Salt and freshly ground
   black pepper
8 flour tortillas
1 Tbsp capers, rinsed
1 handful basil
8oz (250g) taleggio cheese

Preheat the grill pan or grill plate to very hot. Slice the eggplant and zucchinis into ⅛–¼-in (3–5-mm) thick slices. Quarter and deseed the peppers. Brush the vegetables with a little oil and grill for 2–3 minutes on each side or until soft, cooked and browned. When all the vegetables are cooked, set aside to cool then cut up into small cubes, about ½–¾in (1–2cm) square. Season generously with salt and pepper.

Preheat the grill hot plate or grill pan to medium. Lay out a tortilla on a flat surface and evenly spread over a quarter of the vegetable mixture and capers. Tear over a few basil leaves and top with a quarter of the cheese, cut into small cubes. Place a second tortilla on top, then transfer to the pan or grill. Cook for 2–3 minutes on each side or until golden brown and the cheese is starting to ooze. Repeat until all four are cooked, keeping them warm under a clean tea towel or in a very low oven. Cut up into wedges and serve with your favorite relish, Sweet Thai chilli sauce (see page 167) or tomato sauce.

Vegetable and taleggio tortilla toasties

The classic burger

Nostalgic

This is our tried and tested recipe – it's good-tempered, tasty, and the burgers will fill just about every hamburger bun.

Serves 8

2lb 4oz (1kg) **ground beef**
½ **medium-sized sweet, white onion,** finely chopped
1 tsp **Worcestershire sauce**
1 tsp **dry mustard powder**
1 **egg,** whisked
4 Tbsp **fine breadcrumbs**
1 tsp **salt**
½ tsp **freshly cracked pepper**
8 **hamburger buns**

Suggested toppings:
Ketchup, mayonnaise, selection of mustards, lettuce, sliced dill pickles, Cheddar cheese slices, Caramelized onions (see page 168), sliced roasted red beet

Place the beef in a large bowl and add the remaining ingredients. Stir briefly (this is easiest done with your hands), until just combined.

Over-working the mixture will result in a tough burger.

Wet your hands. Shape the mixture into burgers (weigh the first burger to get an idea of size) by quickly flattening the mixture in your hand (about 1in/2cm thick) and smoothing the edges. Season the burgers again.

Preheat the grill or grill pan to medium-hot. Brush the burgers with a little olive oil. Grill the burgers until brown and charred, about 5 minutes. Turn over and grill for a further 2 minutes for a medium-rare burger, or a further 3–4 minutes for a medium burger.

Once the burgers have been flipped over, use the cooler side of the grill to toast the buns – for about 1 minute. Serve immediately with your choice of toppings.

Lamb and mint burgers with mint sauce

Succulent

These are popular with the whole family, young and old.

Serves 4–6

1lb 12oz (800g) **ground lamb**
1 **clove garlic,** crushed
Generous ½ cup (15g) **mint,** chopped
1 **onion,** finely chopped
⅔ cup (50g) **fresh breadcrumbs**
1 **egg**
1½ tsp **ground cumin**
1½ tsp **ground coriander**
1½ tsp **salt**
Freshly ground black pepper
2 tsp **olive oil**
4–6 **large hamburger buns,** halved
Mint sauce (see page 168)
2 **beef tomatoes,** sliced
1 **Bibb or Boston (round) lettuce**

Put the lamb, garlic, mint, onion, breadcrumbs, egg, spices, salt and pepper in a large bowl. Stir briefly until just combined. Shape the mixture into four burgers, about 7oz (200g) each, or six smaller burgers.

Preheat the grill or grill pan to medium-hot. Brush the burgers with a little olive oil and cook for 5–6 minutes on the first side, then turn and cook for a further 3–4 minutes on the second side or until cooked through. Remove the burgers, cover with foil and set aside while you toast the buns.

If you are using a grill, put the buns cut-side down on the hot plate or grill for about 1 minute, or until golden and toasted. Alternatively, put the buns cut-side up under a preheated broiler for about 1 minute, or until golden and toasted. Put the cooked burgers on the bottom bun, top with mint sauce, tomato and lettuce, and cover with the top bun. Serve immediately.

Steak sandwiches with fennel relish

Substantial

Breakfast, lunch or dinner – I could eat one of these at any time of day. Sometimes I'll throw in a poached egg as well.

Serves 4

For the fennel relish:
1 Tbsp **extra virgin olive oil**
1 **onion,** thinly sliced
1 **large fennel bulb,** very thinly sliced
1 **clove garlic,** crushed
4 Tbsp **extra-fine sugar**
1 Tbsp **wholegrain mustard**
2 Tbsp **white wine vinegar or cider vinegar**

4 **sirloin steaks about** ⅝in (1.5cm) **thick**
Salt and freshly ground black pepper
8 **slices sourdough bread,** grilled
Arugula leaves
Rosemary aïoli (see page 170) (optional)

First make the fennel relish. Heat the oil in a non-stick saucepan over medium heat and add the onion, fennel and garlic. Stir until well coated in the oil and the onion and fennel start to soften but not brown. Increase the heat, add the sugar and stir constantly for a further 2–3 minutes or until starting to brown. Stir in the mustard and vinegar and season generously with salt and pepper. When the liquid has evaporated, reduce the heat slightly and leave the mixture to caramelize and darken around the edges, stirring occasionally, for a further 8–12 minutes. Cool.

Preheat the grill or grill pan to very hot. Season the steak generously on both sides and sear for 2–3 minutes on each side or until cooked to your taste. Lay two slices of sourdough bread on each of four serving plates. Place relish on one piece, top with a steak, aïoli (if using) and arugula, season generously, then top with the second slice of bread. Serve immediately.

Steak sandwiches with fennel relish

Flatbreads with lamb and tzatziki

Comforting

Make the dough and freeze it so you will always have flatbreads as an emergency grill standby.

Serves 4

Flatbread dough (see page 171)
4 lamb leg steaks
Salt and freshly ground black pepper, to taste
2½ cups (100g) mixed salad leaves
Tzatziki (see page 169)

Prepare the flatbread dough as directed (see page 171).

Preheat the grill or a large grill pan to very hot. Season and cook the lamb steaks for 3–4 minutes on each side or until cooked to your taste. Set aside to rest.

Wipe down the pan or grill before cooking the flatbread dough. Cook the flatbreads as directed (see page 171). Continue until all the flatbreads are cooked, stacking on top of each other and covering with a tea towel to keep them warm and soften them.

Slice the lamb steaks and lay some meat, salad leaves and Tzatziki on half of each flatbread, then fold in half to eat.

Flatbreads with lamb and tzatziki

Venison burgers with chutney

Unusual

Venison can be delicious paired with fruit, especially the sweet yet spicy Cranberry pear chutney (see page 169).

Serves 4

1lb 2oz (500g) **ground venison**
2 **shallots**, finely chopped
1 **egg**, whisked
½ tsp **salt**
½ tsp **pepper**
4 **hamburger buns**
**Cranberry pear chutney
(see page 169)**, to serve

Suggested additional toppings:
Mayonnaise
Lettuce
8 thin slices **dill pickles**

Place the meat in a large bowl and add the shallots, egg, salt and pepper. Stir briefly (this is easiest done with your hands), just until combined. Over-working the mixture will result in a tough burger.

Wet your hands. Shape the mixture into burgers (you might want to weigh the first burger to get an idea of size) by quickly flattening the mixture in your hand (about 1in/2cm thick) and, using your other hand, smoothing the edges. Season the burgers again with a sprinkling of salt and pepper.

Preheat the grill or grill pan to medium-hot. Lightly oil the grill bars. Grill the burgers until brown and charred, about 5 minutes. Turn over and grill for a further 2 minutes for a medium-rare burger, 3–4 minutes more for a medium burger.

Once the burgers are flipped, use the cooler side of the grill to toast the buns – 1–2 minutes. Serve immediately. To assemble, top the burgers with a few lettuce leaves, slices of pickles, Cranberry pear chutney and mayonnaise.

Chorizo burgers with avocado cream

Spicy

For me, Saturday in London often involves a trip to Borough market for a chorizo burger. I sometimes attempt to recreate the experience at home, serving them with avocado cream.

Serves 4

2 **avocados**
Juice of 1 **lime**
50ml (2fl oz) **sour cream**
Salt and freshly ground
   black pepper
4 **large burger buns**
4 **chorizo sausages (mild**
   or spicy) about 3oz (80g)
   each
1 Tbsp **Marsala**
2 **red onions,** halved and
   thinly sliced
2½ cups (100g) **arugula**

Scoop out the avocado flesh and put it in a food processor or blender together with the lime juice and sour cream and process to a smooth consistency. Season to taste with salt and pepper and set aside.

Heat the grill hot plate or grill pan to medium-hot. First toast the burger buns, flat-side down, for about 20–30 seconds, or until toasted and golden.
Set aside on serving plates, ready to assemble.

Slice the sausages almost in half lengthways, flatten out, and cook for 2–3 minutes on each side or until golden and crispy. Add the Marsala and onions for the last 3 minutes of cooking. The alcohol will evaporate and the onions will soften and color with the chorizo oils.

Spread the buns with avocado cream, top with a chorizo sausage, onions and arugula. Close the buns and serve immediately.

Blue cheese burgers
Sophisticated

There is nothing better than a rich, sophisticated blue cheese burger. The union fulfills indulgent and comfort cravings simultaneously in one simple bite.

Serves 4

1lb 2oz (500g) **ground beef**
1 Tbsp **Dijon mustard**
3 **spring onions**, finely chopped
1 **clove garlic**, crushed
½ tsp **salt**
½ tsp **pepper**
Olive oil, for brushing
3oz (80g) **blue cheese**, sliced into 8 pieces
4 **hamburger buns**

Suggested toppings:
Mayonnaise, Caramelized onions (see page 168), lettuce leaves

In a large bowl, combine the beef with the mustard, spring onions, garlic, salt and pepper. Stir briefly (this is easiest done with your hands), until just combined. Wet your hands and shape the mixture into four burgers, about 4oz (125g) each.

Season the burgers with a sprinkling of salt and pepper.

Preheat the grill or grill pan to medium-hot and brush with oil. Grill the burgers until brown and charred, about 5 minutes. Turn over and grill for a further 2 minutes for a medium-rare burger, or a further 3–4 minutes for a medium burger. When the second side is grilling, place two pieces of cheese on each burger. Grill the buns at the same time. When the cheese has melted and the burgers are cooked through, remove from the grill.

Serve with your choice of toppings.

■ *Any blue cheese will do: Gorgonzola, Stilton or Danish Blue. For a milder blue experience, try Cambozola.*

Blue cheese burgers

Italian-style sandwiches

Italian-style sandwiches

Luscious

If you have some leftover chicken on hand, omit the first six ingredients and bask in the simplicity.

Serves 2

2 **chicken breasts**
1 Tbsp **olive oil**
1 **clove garlic,** crushed
Juice of 1 **lemon**
⅛ tsp **salt**
⅛ tsp **pepper**
1 **red pepper,** cored and cut into 8 **wedges**
Olive oil, for brushing
4 **slices ciabatta or other crusty bread**
Rosemary aïoli (see page 170)
1 **handful arugula leaves**
1 Tbsp **capers**

Combine chicken breasts in a bowl with olive oil, garlic, lemon juice, salt and pepper. Cover and leave to marinate for 20 minutes at room temperature or up to 1 hour in the refrigerator.

Brush the red pepper wedges with olive oil. Preheat the grill or grill pan to very hot. Grill the chicken for 4–6 minutes on each side until cooked through. Meanwhile, grill the red peppers for 2–3 minutes on each side until grill marks appear and skins are slightly charred. Transfer chicken and peppers to a cutting board and thinly slice.

To assemble the sandwiches, place two ciabatta slices on a cutting board. Spread Rosemary aïoli over them, top with chicken, red pepper, arugula and capers, then season with salt and pepper to taste. Cover with the remaining slices of bread and brush with oil. Grill the sandwiches on both sides, pressing gently with a spatula until grill marks appear on the surface of the bread.

Transfer the sandwiches to serving plates, slice in half and serve immediately.

Nutty lentil burgers

Nutty

Thanks go to Jenn Grant, a veggie burger afficionado for this recipe. The burgers are flavorful and stay intact on the grill.

Serves 6

3 Tbsp **olive oil**
½ **medium onion,** finely diced
2 cups (300g) **cooked brown lentils (canned is fine),** drained well
½ cup (50g) **finely chopped walnuts**
2 cups (300g) **cooked brown rice**
2 Tbsp **smooth peanut butter**
1⅓ cups (100g) **dry breadcrumbs**
1 Tbsp **finely chopped parsley**
½ tsp **salt**
⅛ tsp **freshly ground black pepper**

To serve:
6 **whole-wheat rolls,** sliced and toasted
Mayonnaise
6 Tbsp **Peanut sauce (see page 166)**
2 **tomatoes,** thinly sliced
2 cups (20g) **alfalfa sprouts**

Heat 1 Tbsp of the oil in a large frying pan over medium heat. Add the onion, cover and cook, stirring a few times until softened, about 5 minutes. Transfer to a food processor.

Add the lentils, walnuts, rice, peanut butter, breadcrumbs, parsley, salt and pepper to the onion and process to blend well. Turn the mixture out into a bowl and shape into six burgers. Refrigerate for at least 30 minutes.

Heat a grill or grill pan to medium and brush with the remaining oil. Cook the burgers, turning once, until browned on both sides and heated through. Place a burger on the bottom half of each toasted burger roll, top with mayonnaise, Peanut sauce, tomatoes and sprouts, and cover with the other bun half.

Cambozola quesadillas

Oozing

It's natural to want to feature these stellar quesadillas as an appetizer at any grill gathering. But be warned – they will be devoured, and no one will be hungry for the main course.

Makes 12 wedges

7oz (200g) **Cambozola cheese**
4 x 10-in (24-cm) **flour tortillas**
1 **red pepper,** cored and finely sliced
1 **red chilli pepper,** finely chopped
1 **mango,** skin removed and finely sliced
½ **white onion,** finely sliced
4 tsp **chopped cilantro**
Olive oil, for brushing

Preheat the grill or grill pan to very hot.

Spread Cambozola evenly over the tortillas. Scatter sliced red pepper, chilli, mango and onion over half of each tortilla. Sprinkle cilantro over the top. Fold the tortillas in half and brush with olive oil. Grill on both sides until grill marks appear on the surface and the cheese has melted. Transfer the quesadillas to a cutting board and cut into wedges.

■ *Cambozola is a creamy blend of Camembert and blue cheese. Brie, Camembert, Gorgonzola or any other creamy cheese can be substituted.*

Smoky portobello mushroom burger

Earthy

Even the most ardent carnivores will fall in love with this
thick, meaty alternative to traditional burgers.

Serves 4

4 large Portobello
   mushrooms, stems
   removed
Handful of wood chips,
   soaked for 1 hour
   (optional)
4 hamburger buns
   sliced in half

For the marinade:
½ cup (125ml) olive oil
Generous ¼ cup (75ml) red
   wine vinegar
2 Tbsp Dijon mustard
2 cloves garlic, thinly sliced
1 Tbsp fresh thyme
1 Tbsp chopped basil
½ tsp sea salt
⅛ tsp pepper

Suggested toppings:
Mayonnaise, Dijon
   mustard, mature
   Cheddar cheese slices,
   lettuce leaves, sliced
   tomatoes, thinly sliced
   red onion

Place the mushrooms in a
shallow baking dish. In a
small bowl, whisk the
marinade ingredients
together and drizzle over the
mushrooms, turning to coat.
Cover and refrigerate for at
least 30 minutes or up to
3 hours.

Preheat the grill or grill pan to
medium-high heat. Grill the
mushrooms for 3–4 minutes
on each side until browned
and very tender. Toast the
buns on the bars until lightly
toasted.

Place the mushrooms on
the bottom half of the buns.
Top with your chosen
toppings and cover with the
top half of the buns. Serve
immediately.

Smoky portobello mushroom burger

Sweet potato and cilantro quesadillas

Substantial

A recipe from Jolene d'Entrement, who makes these quesadillas for her young but gourmet family. The recipe can be altered – experiment with cheeses, fresh herbs and spices.

Serves 4

1 tsp **olive oil**
1 **onion**, finely chopped
1 **clove garlic**, finely chopped
1 **large sweet potato, about** 15oz (400g), peeled and grated
2 tsp **ground cumin**
½ tsp **dried oregano**
1 tsp **chilli powder**
1 pinch **cayenne pepper**
4 x 9½-in (24-cm) **wide tortillas**
7oz (200g) **havarti cheese,** grated
1 **bunch cilantro,** roughly chopped
Olive oil, for brushing

Heat the oil in a large frying pan over medium heat. Add the finely chopped onion and garlic and sauté until the onions are translucent. Add the grated sweet potato and cook until wilted and cooked through, stirring occasionally. Add the spices and continue to cook for a further 2–3 minutes.

Preheat the grill or grill pan to medium-hot. Spoon the sweet potato mixture onto two tortillas. Top with the grated havarti cheese and chopped cilantro, then cover with the remaining tortillas. Brush the tortillas with olive oil and carefully invert onto the grill. Grill, pressing lightly with a spatula until marks appear on the surface. Brush the tops with olive oil, turn over and grill the other side. Move the quesadillas to indirect heat (or reduce the heat under the grill pan to low) and continue to cook until the cheese has melted. Transfer to a cutting board and cut into wedges. Serve immediately.

Pork sausage pitas with Asian slaw

Simplicity

These are a real hit with both young and old, using a healthy version of the more familiar mayonnaise-based coleslaw.

Serves 4

1½ cups (150g) **finely shredded white or red cabbage**
2 **carrots,** grated
½ cup (50g) **snow peas,** finely sliced lengthwise
2 Tbsp **toasted sesame seeds**
Juice of 1 **lime**
1 Tbsp **fish sauce**
2 Tbsp **light olive oil**
1 Tbsp **kecap manis**
1 Tbsp **extra-fine sugar**
1 tsp **finely grated ginger**
4 **pita pockets**
6 **pork sausages,** halved lengthwise
Gran's plum sauce (see page 167) (optional)

Put the first four ingredients in a large bowl and mix to combine. Whisk together the lime juice, fish sauce, olive oil, kecap manis, sugar and ginger until the sugar has dissolved. Pour over the shredded cabbage mixture, mix well and set aside in the refrigerator for at least 30 minutes. When you are ready to cook the sausages, remove the slaw from the refrigerator and bring back to room temperature.

Heat a grill pan or grill to medium-hot. Place the pita pockets on the grill for about 1–2 minutes on each side, or until toasted and starting to puff. Remove from the heat and slit open one side using a small knife.

Turn the heat to hot and cook the sausage halves, flat side down for 3 minutes, turn and cook for a further 2–3 minutes or until golden brown and cooked through.

Just before serving, pour any extra liquid off the slaw. Serve three sausage halves and a generous spoonful each of slaw and Gran's plum sauce in each pita pocket.

Pizza with tomatoes and chèvre pesto

Pizza with tomatoes and chèvre pesto

Toothsome

Grilling pizza is a fun way to serve up this year-around classic. Be sure to follow the recipe for pizza dough – it's soft, yet dense enough to keep its shape on the grill.

Makes 6 x 8-in (20-cm) pizzas

Pizza base dough (see page 171)
6 plum tomatoes, thinly sliced, or 6 bunches of vine cherry tomatoes, charred if liked
Olive oil, for brushing

For the chèvre pesto:
2 cloves garlic
2 large handfuls basil leaves
4 Tbsp pine nuts, toasted
6–7 Tbsp olive oil
3½oz (100g) soft fresh chèvre (goat's cheese)
Salt and pepper, to taste

Prepare the pizza dough as directed (see page 171).

Make the pesto by combining the garlic, basil and pine nuts in a food processor. Pulse until chopped. Slowly add the oil and pulse until smooth. Add the chèvre and stir with a fork until smooth. Season with salt and pepper. Set aside with the tomatoes.

Preheat the grill to high on one side, warm on the other. Brush one side of the dough with olive oil. Pick up one round of dough with both hands and place oiled-side down, on the hot side of the grill. Grill until grill marks appear on the surface, 2–3 minutes. Flip the dough over and arrange the pesto and tomatoes on the cooked side. When the bottom has browned, slide the pizza to the cooler side of the grill. Close the lid and grill the pizza until the toppings are hot and the cheese has melted. Transfer the pizza to a cutting board and continue with next round of dough. Cut the pizza and serve.

Skewered

My first exposure to meat on a stick wasn't necessarily a gourmet experience. My home town of Halifax, Nova Scotia, is famous for many things, one being the Doner. This is meant to be sliced mutton wrapped with herbs and mounted upon a rotating vertical skewer. The Halifax version, however, is more like grey, spicy Spam. The server slices it off the skewer with a sword, quickly grills the meat, then mounds it over pita. A few chopped tomatoes and pieces of raw onion are thrown in, then – the pièce de resistance – a creamy sauce made with sweetened milk and garlic is added. It's grey, it's gloopy and it's downright delicious.

While I was eating Doners in Halifax, Pippa was at her beach house on Waiheke Island in New Zealand, enjoying skewered prawns fresh from the Pacific. Regardless of our beginnings, our love for all things skewered is equally strong. They appease the appetite, cook quickly and – Doners aside – can easily be enjoyed while simultaneously sipping a glass of wine. What could be better than that?

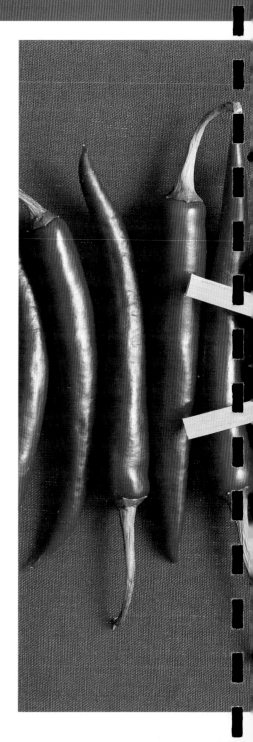

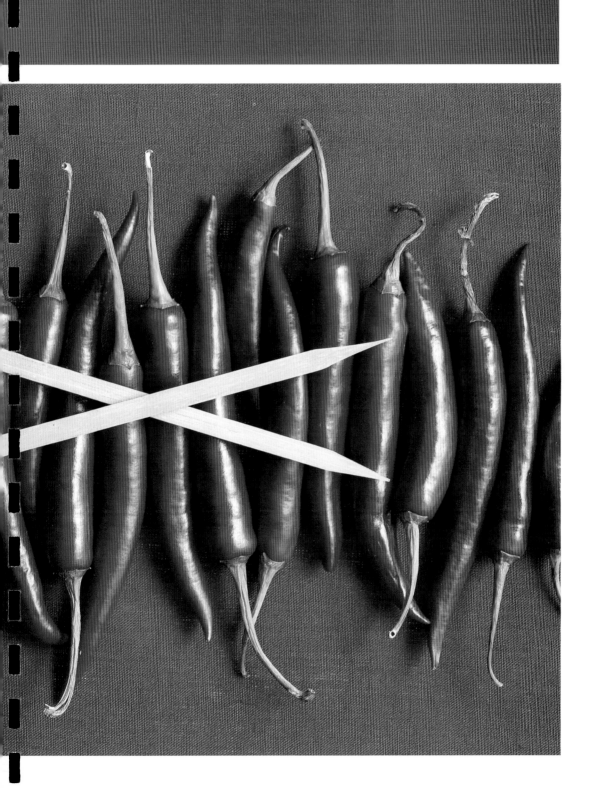

Honey lamb koftas

Succulent

Honey makes these lamb koftas very sweet and juicy. The sweetness perfectly complements the hit from the chilli, which you can adjust to your liking.

Makes 10–12

14oz (400g) minced lamb
1 onion, finely chopped
1 tsp smoked paprika
2 garlic cloves, finely chopped
½ tsp chilli flakes
2 Tbsp runny honey
1 tsp salt
½ cup (10g) mint, roughly chopped
Tzatziki (see page 169), to serve

12 wooden or bamboo skewers, soaked (see page 14)

Put the lamb, onion, paprika, garlic, chilli flakes, honey, salt and mint in a food processor and process until just combined and smooth. Using wet hands, shape the mixture into 10–12 balls. Take each individual portion and shape it on to a soaked skewer to form about a 4-in (10-cm) oblong kofta. Continue until all are done.

Heat the grill or grill pan to medium-hot. Cook the koftas for about 8–10 minutes, turning 2–3 times, or until the lamb is cooked. Serve hot with a generous dollop of Tzatziki.

Monkfish and red onion kebabs

Mediterranean

Monkfish is an excellent choice for kebabs because of its firm, almost meat-like texture. You can also make mini kebabs and serve them as Spanish tapas.

Makes 12

1lb 5oz (600g) **monkfish,** cut into ¾-in (2-cm) **cubes**
4 **red onions,** cut into 6 wedges each
24 **bay leaves,** soaked

For the marinade:
2 **cloves garlic,** crushed
2 tsp **sweet smoked paprika**
Juice of 1 **lemon**
2 **sprigs thyme,** leaves only
2 Tbsp **extra virgin olive oil**
Freshly ground black pepper
Extra lemon wedges, to serve

12 **wooden or bamboo skewers,** soaked (see page 14)

Hold a bamboo skewer with one hand and thread on the ingredients in the following order: monkfish, onion wedge, bay leaf, monkfish, onion wedge, bay leaf, monkfish. Set aside in a long, high-sided dish while you make the marinade.

Combine the crushed garlic, paprika, lemon juice, thyme sprigs, olive oil and ground black pepper in a bowl and whisk with a fork to combine. Pour over the kebabs and turn to coat. Leave the kebabs to marinate for 30 minutes up to overnight in the fridge, turning occasionally.

Remove the kebabs from the fridge 30 minutes before cooking and preheat the grill or grill pan to medium-hot. Cook the kebabs for about 6–8 minutes, turning occasionally until the fish is golden and cooked through. Serve immediately with lemon wedges to squeeze over on the side.

Shrimp and chorizo skewers

Spanish

All the juices and oils from the chorizo ooze out while cooking, leaving the shrimp succulent and spicy.

Makes 12

12 **large shrimp**
1 Tbsp **harissa paste (optional)**
2 **chorizo sausages**, about 6oz (150g) **each**
12 **fresh bay leaves**
1 Tbsp **olive oil**
12 **short skewers**, soaked in wood or bamboo

Peel and devein the shrimp, leaving the small tail ends still attached. Rub over the harissa paste evenly and set aside. Slice the chorizo into ½-in (1½-cm) thick slices. Place 1 chorizo slice into the crook of each shrimp and thread onto a skewer. Add a bay leaf to each skewer and refrigerate until ready to cook.

Preheat the grill or grill pan to medium-hot. Brush the skewers with a little olive oil and cook for 5–6 minutes, turning once, or until the shrimp are translucent and the chorizo cooked through. Serve immediately.

Shrimp and chorizo skewers

Peri-peri butterflied chicken

Spicy

This is a definite favorite for men – I think they just enjoy getting their fingers dirty and the real hit of chilli. Cooking it on the grill is definitely preferred. It becomes crispy and almost charred in parts from the flames.

Serves 4

1 **medium chicken, about** 3lb (1.3kg), **butterflied** (see page 19)
2–3 **red chilli peppers,** stems removed and roughly chopped
Juice of 2 **lemons, about** 4 Tbsp
4 Tbsp **olive oil**
1 Tbsp **cayenne pepper**
2 **cloves garlic,** crushed
1 Tbsp **smoked paprika**
1 tsp **salt**

Butterfly the chicken. Insert a metal skewer horizontally through the wings and breast. Push a second metal skewer horizontally through the thighs. Set aside until the marinade is ready.

Put the chilli peppers, lemon juice, oil, cayenne, garlic, paprika and salt in a food processor or blender and process to a smooth paste. Place half the marinade in a large flat dish. Put the chicken on top and pour over the remaining marinade, ensuring that it covers both sides. Cover and refrigerate for at least 30 minutes or up to 24 hours.

Preheat the grill to hot. Cook, bone-side down for 15–20 minutes, reducing the heat if necessary. Turn the chicken over and cook skin-side down for a further 15–20 minutes, depending on the size of the bird, or until the skin is brown and crispy but not burned. Cook until no pink juices run from the meat when a skewer is inserted into the thigh. When the bird is cooked leave it to rest, covered, for 5 minutes. Cut into four pieces and serve.

Peri-peri butterflied chicken

Spicy chicken satay skewers

Fragrant

These grilled skewers are equally delicious made with beef. Serve them with our Peanut sauce (see page 166) and don't forget to soak your skewers first.

Makes 12

1lb 5oz (600g) **chicken breasts,** cut into ¾-in (2-cm) cubes or into strips
1 **onion,** finely chopped
1 **stalk lemongrass,** finely sliced
1 **clove garlic,** chopped
1-in (2.5-cm) **piece fresh ginger,** finely chopped
1 tsp **ground coriander**
1 tsp **ground cumin**
½ tsp **ground turmeric**
½ tsp **salt**
1 tsp **brown sugar**
1 Tbsp **soy sauce**
3 Tbsp **crunchy peanut butter**
Juice of 1 **lime**
1 Tbsp **peanut or sunflower oil**
Peanut sauce (see page 166), to serve

12 **wooden or bamboo skewers,** soaked (see page 14)

Thread about five to six cubes or two strips of chicken onto each skewer and set aside in a dish.

To make the satay mixture, put all the remaining ingredients (except the Peanut sauce) into a food processor and process until everything is well blended and smooth. Pour the satay mixture over the chicken, using your hands to ensure it covers all the surfaces, then cover and marinate in the refrigerator for 1–2 hours or overnight.

When you are ready to cook, preheat the grill or grill pan to medium-hot. Cook for 8–12 minutes, turning frequently, or until cooked through and no pink juices run when cut. Serve with Peanut sauce.

Spicy chicken satay skewers

Dalmatian scallop shish kebabs

Coastal

This recipe comes from Vjekica Sucic Hruskovec, a Croatian friend who now lives in Canada. Her father used to make these kebabs for the family on summer holidays in Split, on the Dalmatian coast.

Serves 4 as a starter

For the marinade:
1 Tbsp **fresh rosemary,** finely chopped
1 **bay leaf**
1 tsp **whole peppercorns**
2 Tbsp **red wine vinegar**
1 cup (250ml) **orange juice**
1 tsp **orange zest**
1 tsp **honey**
Pinch **salt**

For the shish kebab:
16 **large, fresh scallops**
8 slices **prosciutto,** cut in half
4 **Clementine oranges,** quartered
1 **red or yellow pepper,** cored and chopped into 1½in (4cm) cubes
Vegetable oil, for brushing

4 x 12-in (30-cm) **skewers,** soaked for 30 minutes if wooden

Combine the marinade ingredients in a small saucepan and bring to a boil. Simmer gently for 3 minutes, then remove from heat and cool.

Wrap half a slice of the prosciutto around scallops. Thread four of the orange segments, wrapped scallops and peppers onto each skewer. Place skewers in a shallow dish and pour over marinade. Leave to infuse for 10 minutes at room temperature.

Meanwhile, preheat a grill or grill pan to medium heat and brush with oil. Grill the kebabs for 4–5 minutes per side, until prosciutto is crispy and orange skins begin to char. Baste with marinade.

Serve immediately, squeezing orange wedges over the scallops and peppers.

Korean beef with cherry tomatoes

Sweet

This recipe is based on Bulgogi, Korea's famous grilled beef dish traditionally marinated in soy sauce. Like soy sauce, kiwi fruit is also an incredible meat tenderizer. It has the ability to transform tougher cuts such as flank steak into tender meat.

Serves 4 as a starter

For the marinade:
2 Tbsp **rice wine vinegar**
2 Tbsp **soy sauce**
1 Tbsp **brown sugar**
2 tsp **sesame oil**
1 **clove garlic,** crushed
1 tsp **very finely chopped fresh ginger**
½ **kiwi fruit,** skin removed and the flesh mashed with a fork

10oz (300g) **flank steak**
16 **cherry tomatoes**
8 **soft lettuce leaves, e.g. Bibb or Boston (round)**
1 Tbsp **sesame seeds,** toasted, to garnish

8 **small bamboo skewers,** soaked (see page 14)

Combine the ingredients for the marinade and pour into a shallow dish. Slice the steak into ¾-in (2-cm) cubes, about 16 in total. Add the steak to the marinade and toss to coat. Leave to marinate for 20 minutes. Thread beef and cherry tomatoes alternately onto skewers, two of each per skewer.

Meanwhile, preheat the grill or grill pan to medium-hot and lightly oil. Grill the skewers for 4–5 minutes on each side until the tomatoes begin to collapse and the beef is charred and cooked through.

Serve the skewers over lettuce leaves and sprinkle with sesame seeds.

Lamb skewers with rosemary
Tender

Creamy plain yogurt is an excellent meat tenderizer. Add a little garlic, fresh rosemary and a hot grill and voilà!

Serves 4

1lb 2-oz (500-g) **piece boneless leg or shoulder of lamb**

For the marinade:
Scant ½ cup (100ml) **full-fat plain yogurt**
2 **cloves garlic,** thinly sliced
1 Tbsp **finely chopped rosemary**
½ tsp **ground black pepper**
1 tsp **salt**

For the rosemary salt:
1 tsp **finely chopped fresh rosemary**
1 tsp **coarse sea salt**

To serve:
Boiled new potatoes
Green salad

Cut the lamb into 1-in (2.5-cm) square cubes and place in a shallow dish.

Combine the yogurt, garlic, rosemary, pepper and salt. Pour over the lamb cubes, turning to coat. Cover and refrigerate, tossing occasionally, for 5 hours. Thread the lamb cubes onto four metal skewers and bring to room temperature, about 30 minutes.

For the rosemary salt, combine the ingredients and set aside.

Preheat the grill or grill pan to medium-hot and brush with oil. Grill the skewers for 2–3 minutes on all four sides until the lamb is cooked through. Remove the skewers from the grill and allow to rest.

Place the lamb cubes on a serving plate. Sprinkle with rosemary salt and serve with boiled new potatoes and a green salad.

Lesley's killer jerk chicken

Resonant

"Jerk" ingredients vary, depending on the cook. This version comes from Lesley, a friend who makes the best jerk around.

Serves 4–6

For the jerk marinade:
1 **onion,** finely chopped
6 **spring onions,** finely chopped
2 tsp **dried thyme**
1 tsp **salt**
2 tsp **sugar**
1 tsp **allspice**
½ tsp **grated nutmeg**
½ tsp **cinnamon**
¼ tsp **cayenne pepper**
1 tsp **ground black pepper**
3 Tbsp **soy sauce**
1 Tbsp **olive oil**
1 Tbsp **cider or white vinegar**

2lb 4oz (1kg) **boneless chicken breasts or thighs,** chopped into 1¼-in (3-cm) **squares**

For the dipping sauce:
1 cup (250ml) **Greek yogurt**
1lb 5oz (600g) **cucumber,** finely chopped
1 Tbsp **cider vinegar**
½ tsp **salt**

1 pinch cayenne pepper
1 Tbsp **Dijon mustard**
1 **clove garlic,** finely chopped

8 **wooden skewers,** soaked for 1 hour (see page 14)

Combine the ingredients for the marinade in a large bowl and toss with the chicken. Cover and marinate for 24 hours.

For the dipping sauce, combine all the ingredients. Cover with plastic wrap and chill until needed, up to 24 hours.

Preheat the grill or grill pan to medium-hot and brush with oil. Thread the chicken onto skewers and place on the grill. Grill for 3–4 minutes on each side until cooked through. Serve the skewers with dipping sauce on the side.

Yakitori

Yakitori

Insatiable

Yakitori refers to grilled chicken skewers, Japanese-style. The yakitori repertoire extends far beyond the realms of chicken, however. Here are two favorites.

Each recipe makes 6 x
6-in (15-cm) skewers

**For the master sauce for
all Yakitori:**
½ cup (125ml) **soy sauce**
½ cup (125ml) **mirin or dry
sherry**
1 Tbsp **brown sugar**

In a saucepan whisk together the soy sauce, mirin and sugar and bring the mixture to a boil over moderate heat. Simmer for 5 minutes, or until the sugar is dissolved and the mixture begins to thicken. Set aside.

Chicken and spring onion yakitori:
4 **skinless, boneless
chicken thighs,** cut into
18 x 1¼-in (3-cm) cubes
5 **spring onions, white and
pale green parts only,**
cut into 12 x 1¼in
(3-cm) lengths

Quail's egg yakitori
18 **quail's eggs,** hard-
boiled and shelled

6 x 6-in (15-cm) **wooden
skewers,** soaked for
1 hour (see page 14)

Thread the chicken and spring onion onto skewers, three pieces of chicken per skewer, or thread three quail eggs onto each skewer.

Preheat the grill or grill pan to hot. Brush the skewers with master sauce. Grill the chicken skewers for 2–3 minutes on each side, until cooked through. The quail eggs only need 1 minute per side. Baste the skewers liberally with the master sauce while grilling. Serve immediately with extra sauce for dipping.

Salads and vegetables

One can't deny the attraction of men to barbecue. They can eat with their fingers, throw a ball and sit in the sun, simultaneously. Beer is encouraged and setting food on fire is not only alright, it's expected.

But, let's face it. Grills just aren't as masculine as they used to be. Steaks are now sharing the grill with asparagus spears, prosciutto-wrapped peaches and halloumi cheese. Chicory (endive) is moving in, pumpkin is taking over, and eggplants? They deserve a grill all to themselves.

Australian-born food writer Terry Durack addressed this phenomenon in an article he wrote. No longer are barbecues "slash and burn" affairs where men drink "cold tinnies and eat cremated lamb chops." Instead, the tinny is more likely to be "a well-chilled Claire Riesling or Yarra Valley Pinot Noir. Blimey, we even use glasses."

I believe strength is measured by one's ability to handle delicate situations. So men, it's time to reach for those vegetables and tighten the aprons, because it looks like grilled salads are here to stay.

Chargrilled squash and sesame salad

Soy-sweet

This salad is superb served with plain chicken breasts and green beans. Make it a day in advance; the flavor gets better and better.

Serves 4

1 large butternut squash or pumpkin, about 2lb 4oz (1kg)
1½ Tbsp olive oil

For the dressing:
1 tsp sesame oil
2 Tbsp sesame seeds
1 Tbsp miso paste
2 Tbsp soy sauce
2 Tbsp runny honey
2 spring onions, sliced to serve

Peel the butternut squash and cut into thin slices, about ⅟₁₆-in (2-mm) thick. Coat the squash slices in oil and set aside.

Heat the sesame oil in a small saucepan and toast the sesame seeds for about 2 minutes or until golden and starting to pop. Remove from the heat and stir in the miso paste, soy sauce and honey. Return to the heat, bring back to a boil and simmer for a further minute. Remove from the heat, stir in the spring onions and set aside while you cook the butternut squash.

Preheat the grill or grill pan to hot. Cook the squash in a single layer for about 2 minutes on each side, or until soft and cooked. Put the cooked squash on a serving plate while you cook the rest. When all the squash is cooked, pour over the slightly cooled dressing and gently mix. Serve warm or leave to cool.

Halloumi and grilled lemon salad

Simplicity

Halloumi cheese is a great alternative to meat when you have vegetarians for dinner. Here the halloumi is marinated in harissa paste.

Serves 4

1½ Tbsp **harissa paste**
1½ Tbsp **extra virgin olive oil, plus extra to serve**
10oz (300g) **halloumi cheese,** cut into about 12 slices about ½-in (1-cm) thick
4 **lemons,** halved
5 cups (200g) **arugula**
Freshly ground black pepper

Combine the harissa paste and olive oil and use to evenly coat the halloumi slices. Cover and refrigerate for 4 hours or overnight.

When you are ready to serve, heat the grill or grill pan to hot. Grill the halloumi slices for about 2–3 minutes on each side, or until grill marks form on the surface and the cheese is warmed through.

Rub the cut side of the lemons into the remaining harissa marinade and grill, cut-side down for 3–4 minutes or until dark and fragrant. When cooked, put three halloumi slices and two lemon halves on each plate and top with a handful of arugula leaves. Drizzle with a little extra virgin olive oil and lots of freshly ground black pepper. Encourage your guests to squeeze the lemon over the salad before eating. Serve immediately.

Grilled zucchini and mint salad
Spring-like

The best version of this salad is the one Ursula Ferrigno makes. It calls for the long task of drying the zucchini slices in the sun or oven first before grilling them. It's well worth the effort if you have the time. This version is for those of us who never seem to have enough time.

Serves 4–6

6 **zucchinis, about** 2lb 4oz (1kg) **in total,** sliced lengthways into ⅟₁₆-in (1–2-mm) **thick slices**
2 Tbsp **extra virgin olive oil**

For the dressing:
Juice of 1 **lemon**
3 Tbsp **extra virgin olive oil**
1 **clove garlic,** crushed
½ cup (10g) **mint, chopped** plus extra to garnish
Salt and freshly ground black pepper
¾ cup (50g) **pine nuts, toasted** (optional)

Heat the grill or grill pan to medium-hot. Brush the zucchini slices with a little olive oil and put as many as you can in a single layer on the grill or grill pan. Leave to cook for 1–2 minutes on each side, or until charred and cooked. Remove and set aside, repeating until all the slices are cooked. Leave the zucchini slices to cool slightly while you prepare the dressing.

Whisk the lemon juice, olive oil, garlic and mint together and season generously with salt and pepper. Pour the dressing over the still warm zucchinis and gently combine.

This salad can be served warm or left to marinate for up to 24 hours. Just before serving top with extra mint and toasted pine nuts, if liked.

■ *Use a mandolin cutter to slice the zucchinis if you have one. It produces very thin slices.*

Grilled zucchini and mint salad

Fattoush

Fresh

This Lebanese bread salad is so simple it makes for a perfect quick lunch or light supper accompaniment.

Serves 4

2–3 **soft flour tortillas**
2 Tbsp **olive oil**

For the dressing:
3 Tbsp **red wine vinegar**
4 Tbsp **extra virgin olive oil**
1 tsp **sumac**
Sea salt and freshly ground black pepper
4 **red, green or yellow tomatoes,** cut into ½–¾-in (1–2-cm) cubes
1 **large** or 2 **small cucumbers,** halved lengthways then cut into ½–¾-in (1–2-cm) chunks
1 **red onion,** cut into ½-in (1-cm) chunks
1 **small handful mint,** torn
1 **small handful flat-leaf parsley,** torn

Preheat the grill or grill pan to medium-hot. While heating, brush the tortillas generously on both sides with oil. Put the tortillas, one at a time, on the grill or in the grill pan and cook for about 1 minute on the first side and about 30 seconds – 1 minute on the second side. Remove the tortillas and leave to cool while you prepare the dressing.

In a small bowl combine the vinegar, oil and sumac with a fork and season generously with salt and pepper. Put the cubed tomato, cucumber and red onion in a salad bowl. Break the tortillas into the salad and add the herbs. Pour over the dressing and toss to combine. Serve immediately while the tortillas are still crispy.

Fattoush

Asparagus wrapped in prosciutto

Effective

The saltiness of the ham and the sweetness of the asparagus, when it is in season, is a match made in heaven. Asparagus grilled on its own is a delicious vegetarian alternative.

Serves 4–6

24 **asparagus spears**
5oz (150g) (about 12) **prosciutto slices,** halved
Extra virgin olive oil
Freshly ground black pepper

Snap the ends off the asparagus where they break naturally and trim the ends on a diagonal.

Wrap half a slice of prosciutto around the center of each asparagus spear. Preheat the grill or grill pan to medium-hot and cook all the asparagus spears at once, drizzle over a little oil while cooking and season with plenty of freshly ground black pepper, for about 3–4 minutes, turning once or twice. The ham will go crispy and golden brown and the asparagus will turn bright green. Serve hot, warm or cold.

■ *These can be served as a side dish or as a starter. Have a bowl of Rosemary aïoli (see page 170) on the side for guests to dip them into as finger-food.*

Asparagus wrapped in prosciutto

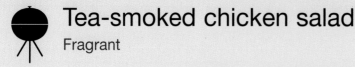

Tea-smoked chicken salad

Fragrant

If you don't own a proper smoker then this is the cheat's way to achieve a very similar result.

Serves 4–6

½ cup (75g) **Assam or any other tea leaves**
½ cup (75g) **brown sugar**
½ cup (75g) **basmati rice**
4 **skinless, boneless chicken breasts**
Salt and freshly ground black pepper
2 tsp **olive oil**
1 cup (200g) **canned artichoke hearts,** drained and halved
1 **red onion,** sliced
⅓ cup (50g) **preserved lemon slices**
20 cups (200g) **salad leaves**

For the dressing:
Juice of 1 **lemon**
2 Tbsp **extra virgin olive oil**
1 Tbsp **thyme leaves**
Salt and freshly ground black pepper

Mix together the tea leaves, sugar and rice. Line the base and sides of a large, old roasting dish with foil. Sprinkle the tea mixture over the foil and place a metal rack into the dish that sits high enough not to touch the mixture.

Season the chicken breasts and drizzle over the oil. Lay the chicken flat on the wire rack and cover loosely, so the foil doesn't touch the chicken, with a further three layers of foil. Set the roasting dish over very hot embers or a very hot grill plate on your grill. When the dish starts smoking leave it for a further 10 minutes. Then remove and leave to rest for 5 minutes.

Whisk the dressing ingredients together in a small bowl. Combine the artichoke, onion, lemon and salad leaves in a large bowl and toss well with the dressing and slices of the chicken. Serve immediately.

Eggplant, feta and almond salad

Textural

We like serving this salad with barbecued lamb or beef. Use mint in the salad if you are serving it with lamb, and cilantro if serving it with beef, for the perfect match.

Serves 4–6

3 **large eggplants,** halved
2 Tbsp **olive oil**
1 **garlic clove,** crushed
1 **red chilli,** deseeded and finely diced
Juice of 1 **lemon**
¼ cup (50ml) **extra virgin olive oil**
Sea salt and freshly ground black pepper
3½oz (100g) **feta**
Scant ¾ cup (100g) **whole almonds (skin on),** toasted
1 **small bunch mint or cilantro leaves,** chopped

Preheat the grill or grill pan to medium-hot. Brush the cut surface of the eggplants with oil and cook for 20–30 minutes, turning frequently, until soft, mushy and brown, but still holding their shape. Reduce the heat to medium after 5 minutes.

Cut four of the eggplant halves into cubes and transfer to a medium bowl. Mash the flesh of the remaining two halves using a fork, and add the garlic, chilli, lemon juice, oil, salt and pepper. Add the puréed mixture to the cubes and mix gently until combined.

When ready to serve, place the eggplant mixture on a flat plate or serving dish. Crumble over the feta and finally scatter over the almonds and mint or cilantro. Serve this salad warm to get the best flavor.

Eggplants with pomegranate

Tart

It wasn't until we began working at the London bookshop Books for Cooks that pomegranate molasses became part of our culinary repertoire. Once you start, there's no turning back!

Serves 4

4 **baby eggplants about**
   3½oz (100g) **each or**
   1 **large eggplant**
Olive oil, for brushing
Salt and pepper, to taste
2½ cups (100g) **baby**
   spinach
2oz (50g) **feta cheese**
   (optional)
1 Tbsp **pine nuts,** toasted
2 Tbsp **finely chopped mint**
1 **pomegranate,** seeds
   removed and set aside,
   flesh discarded

For the dressing:
2 heaped Tbsp **plain yogurt**
½ tsp **ground cumin**
1 Tbsp **pomegranate**
   molasses
½ tsp **extra-fine sugar**
1 tsp **lemon juice**

Heat the grill or grill pan to medium-hot. Slice the eggplants into ½-in (1-cm) thick circles and brush with olive oil. Grill until the surface is crisp, the centers are soft and grill marks appear on the surface. Transfer to a plate and sprinkle with salt and pepper. Leave to cool.

Arrange the spinach on a platter and top with eggplant, feta (if using), pine nuts, mint and pomegranate seeds.

In a small bowl, whisk the dressing ingredients together and drizzle over the salad.

■ *Pomegranate molasses is a syrup made from the juices of sour, not sweet, pomegranate seeds. The juice is boiled down to a thick syrup and used often in Iranian cooking. Look for it in Middle Eastern grocers.*

Eggplants with pomegranate

Grilled antipasti

Grilled antipasti

Fresh

This dish is as much a grilled salad as it is an antipasti. Serve warm, hot off the grill, or at room temperature with crusty bread – either grilled or fresh. It is also a delicious accompaniment to grilled chicken, fish or meats – even the humble hamburger.

Serves 4–6

1–2 **eggplants, about** 9oz (500g) sliced into ½-in (1-cm) **rings**
3 **plum tomatoes**
2 **zucchinis, green and yellow,** sliced into rings
1 **red pepper**
1 **yellow pepper**
1 **large onion,** peeled and sliced into ½-in (1-cm) rings
2 **cloves garlic**
Olive oil, for brushing
2 Tbsp **red wine vinegar**
4 Tbsp **capers,** drained and rinsed
1 **handful basil,** roughly chopped
1 **handful flat-leaf parsley,** roughly chopped
1 tsp **sugar**
Salt and pepper, to taste

Preheat the grill or grill pan to hot.

Place the eggplant slices on a cooling rack or in a colander and sprinkle with salt. Leave for 30 minutes, then rinse and pat dry with paper towel. Salting the eggplants in this way draws out all the bitter juices.

Brush the eggplant slices, tomatoes, zucchinis, peppers, onion and garlic with oil. With a large bowl on hand, grill the vegetables in batches until softened and grill marks appear.

Transfer the vegetables to a cutting board, roughly chop and place in a bowl. Add the remaining ingredients, toss and leave to cool and infuse at room temperature for 30 minutes.

Chicory, walnut and pear salad

Sweet

This is delicious with a bit of blue cheese crumbled over the top or a handful of arugula leaves thrown in too. Try red chicory for a bit of added color, or apple for a bit more crunch. This is just a starting point.

Serves 4–6

2–3 heads chicory or endive
¼ cup (50ml) + 1 Tbsp extra virgin olive oil
2–3 ripe pears
Juice of 2 lemons
Salt and freshly ground black pepper
¾ cup (75g) walnuts, toasted

Cut the ends of the chicory and pull the leaves to separate them. Put the chicory in a bowl with 1 Tbsp oil and toss to coat.

Heat the grill hot plate or grill pan to medium and cook the chicory, turning frequently for 2–3 minutes or until wilted and slightly charred. Transfer to a serving plate and leave to cool slightly while you prepare the rest of the salad.

Cut the pears in half, then core and slice thinly. Combine the lemon juice, ¼ cup (50ml) extra virgin olive oil, salt and pepper and pour over the pears. Toss gently to coat and stop browning. Pour the pears and all of the dressing over the chicory. Sprinkle over the walnuts and an extra grinding of black pepper and serve.

Chicory, walnut and pear salad

Grilled chicken, papaya and chilli salad

Hot-sour, salty sweet

This salad is a tribute to Som Tum, the green papaya salad enjoyed all over Thailand. The addition of thinly sliced grilled chicken transforms it into a substantial version of the original.

Serves 4–6

1lb (450g) **skinless, boneless chicken breasts or thighs**
Vegetable oil, for brushing
14oz (400g) **green papaya, finely sliced**
4 Tbsp **palm or brown sugar**
4 Tbsp **fish sauce**
⅔ cup (150ml) **lime or lemon juice**
4 **cloves garlic**
1 cup (100g) **peanuts, roasted**
Scant ¾ cup (100g) **green beans**, cut into 1-in (2.5-cm) lengths
1 **red "finger" chilli pepper,** chopped (optional)
2 cups (200g) **cherry tomatoes**, halved

Preheat the grill or grill pan to medium-hot. Brush the chicken with oil and grill for 3–4 minutes on each side. Cool then roughly chop.

Peel the skin off the papaya, scoop out the seeds and julienne the flesh. In a small bowl, blend the palm sugar, fish sauce and lemon or lime juice until the sugar has dissolved. Using a large pestle and mortar or a food processor, pound the garlic cloves with the roasted peanuts until well smashed. Add the papaya, sugar mixture, green beans and chilli, if using, and gently pound until slightly bruised. Place in a large bowl. Add the cherry tomatoes and chicken and stir until everything is combined. Leave the salad to infuse for 15 minutes before serving.

■ *Finely sliced cabbage, cucumber or firm mango can be substituted for the green papaya, or, for a sweeter version of the salad, use ripe papaya.*

Grilled chicken, papaya and chilli salad

Grilled corn on the cob with lime butter

Grilled corn on the cob with lime butter

Seasonal

Corn and limes, when tossed together, make for a sweet, yet pleasingly tart harmony.

Serves 4

For the lime butter:
1¼ sticks (150g) **butter,** softened
Finely grated rind of 2 **limes**
Freshly ground black pepper, to taste
Sea salt, to taste

4 **corn cobs,** husks on

Prepare the lime butter well in advance. Put the butter, lime rind, pepper and salt in a food processor and pulse until well blended. Lay out a large piece of foil, about 10-in (25-cm) square, on a flat surface and put the butter in a log shape in the center. Roll up the foil, shaping the butter into an even log shape, and twist the ends to secure it. Refrigerate the butter for at least 4 hours or, if time is limited, freeze for about 45 minutes. If cutting the butter from frozen, make sure you warm the knife slightly first.

Preheat the grill or grill pan to medium.

Peel back the husks from the corn cobs (do not remove) and discard the silks. Replace the husks and soak in cold water for 10–15 minutes.

Place the corn directly on the grill and cook, turning 2–3 times, for 25 minutes. Allow to cool slightly. Peel back the husks and discard. Serve the corn cobs with the lime butter.

Chicken with spring onion vinaigrette
Smoky

Christa Douglas, my vivacious cooking partner at cooking school in Toronto, came up with this wonderful vinaigrette.

Serves 4

2–3 skinless, boneless
    chicken breasts
3 Tbsp olive oil
Juice of ½ lemon
2 cloves garlic, finely sliced
5 cups (200g) baby spinach
1 avocado, skin removed
    and sliced

For the vinaigrette:
4 spring onions, roots and
    green ends removed
1 clove garlic
½ cup (125ml) extra virgin
    olive oil
Scant ½ cup (100ml) cider
    vinegar
1 Tbsp Dijon mustard
1 Tbsp sugar
¼ tsp salt
Pepper, to taste

Put the chicken in a shallow dish and cover with olive oil, lemon juice and garlic, turning to coat. Set aside.

Preheat the grill or grill pan to medium. Toss the spring onions and garlic with 1 tsp olive oil and grill until grill marks appear. Remove from heat and set aside.

Grill the chicken for 3–4 minutes on each side until cooked through. Remove from the heat, allow to cool then slice across the grain.

Put the spring onions and garlic in a food processor and pulse until chopped. Add the vinegar, mustard, sugar, salt and pepper and purée until smooth. With the motor running, slowly add the remaining oil until well blended. Toss the spinach, chicken and avocado in the vinaigrette.

Grilled sweet potato and mango salad

Pure

A sweet, succulent and refreshing salad.

Serves 4–6

1 **sweet potato,** peeled
1 **large mango,** skin
  removed

For the dressing:
3 Tbsp **olive oil**
4 Tbsp **fresh mint,**
  chopped
Juice of 1 **lime**
1 tsp **grated lime rind**
1 Tbsp **rice wine vinegar**
½ tsp **extra-fine sugar**
Sea salt and pepper, to
  taste

1 head **Bibb or Boston
  (round) lettuce**
½ cup (10g) **fresh mint**

Preheat the grill or grill pan
to medium.

Chop both the sweet potato
and mango flesh into long
wedges, about ¾-in (2cm)
wide, ½-in (1cm) thick. Place
in separate dishes.

Combine the dressing
ingredients in a small bowl
and pour half over the
mango and potato.

With tongs in hand, arrange
sweet potato wedges
directly over the grill and
leave for 6–8 minutes, until
grill marks appear and the
bottom sides begin to
soften. Turn and grill the
other side for a further
6 minutes. While the other
sides are cooking, arrange
the mango wedges directly
on the grill. Grill for about
2–3 minutes on each side.
Transfer all the wedges to
a cutting board and cut
into cubes. Place them in
a bowl and toss with the
remaining dressing.

Arrange lettuce leaves on
salad plates. Scatter the
sweet potato and mango
over the lettuce and add a
sprinkling of sea salt and
finely sliced mint.

Smoked vegetarian Caesar salad

Sharp

I first tasted a "smoked" Caesar salad at a Halifax restaurant called Seven. They have a wood-fired oven, which flavors the lettuce rather than cooking it. I couldn't wait to get home, light up the coals and give it a try. A grill pan, although it doesn't lend a smoky flavor, will work just fine.

Serves 4

For the Caesar dressing:
3½oz (100g) **silken tofu**
2 Tbsp **lemon juice**
2 tsp **Dijon mustard**
1 clove **garlic,** crushed
¼ tsp **salt**
1 pinch **sugar**
Dash **Worcestershire sauce**
2 Tbsp **grated Parmesan**
Freshly ground pepper, to
    taste

For the crispy capers:
2 Tbsp **olive oil**
¾ cup (50g) **capers**

2 **heads Cos or Romaine
    lettuce,** outer leaves
    removed
Parmesan shavings, to
    garnish

1 **handful wood chips,**
    soaked for 1 hour

To make the dressing, put all ingredients into a blender and blend until smooth.

For the crispy capers, pour the olive oil into a small saucepan and heat until hot. Add the capers and sauté until crispy. Drain the capers on paper towel.

Preheat the grill or grill pan to medium-hot. If using a grill, scatter wood chips over the coals or place in a smoker box. Brush the grill with oil. Grill the lettuce halves, cut-side down, until warm and slightly charred, about 2 minutes. Divide between four salad plates. Top with dressing, crispy capers and shavings of Parmesan.

■ *Use a vegetable peeler to "shave" the Parmesan.*

Smoked vegetarian Caesar salad

Scallop and broccoli stir-fry
Smoky-sweet

When not making music videos, friend and charcoal afficionado Colin MacKenzie can be found in his back garden, grilling for the myriad rockers who come through his door. Colin likes to whip up this quick stir-fry to appease the masses while the main event cooks away. A grill basket is essential to create a smoky, charred effect.

Serves 2–3

1 **handful wood chips,** soaked for at least 30 minutes

Juice of 1 **lime**
2 tsp **sesame oil**
½ tsp **chilli paste**
1 pinch **brown sugar**
1 head **broccoli florets,** separated and stalk discarded
7oz (200g) **fresh scallops**
Salt and pepper, to taste

Preheat the grill to medium-hot. Add the wood chips, either directly over the coals or into the gas grill smoker box. If you don't have a smoker box, use a foil package (see page 15).

Toss the lime juice, 1 tsp of the sesame oil, the chilli paste and brown sugar in a bowl. Add the broccoli florets, toss, and place in a grill basket. Put the basket on the grill bars and sauté the broccoli florets using tongs, until lightly charred.

Toss the scallops in the remaining lime juice and sesame oil and add to the broccoli. Continue to sauté until the scallops are crispy around the edges and just cooked through, about 1–2 minutes, depending on their size.

Season with salt and pepper to taste. Serve straight from the grill.

Onions on the grill

Simple

Onion rings are gently steamed and browned, while whole onions, steamed in their own juices, become meltingly tender. Either are the perfect accompaniments to a campfire meal or a gourmet urban barbecue.

Serves 2 (onion rings)
Serves 1 (whole onion)

For onion rings:
1 **large white onion,** peeled and sliced into ½-in (1-cm) thick rings
1 tsp **olive oil**
Salt and pepper, to taste

Place the onion rings in the center of a 12-in (30-cm) piece of heavy-duty foil. Drizzle with olive oil and season with salt and pepper. Toss. Bring the ends of the foil together and loosely fold. Place on a medium grill and leave to cook for 20–30 minutes or until the onion rings are tender.

For whole onions:
1 tsp **butter**
Salt and pepper, to taste
1 **medium white onion,** peeled

Place the butter in the center of a 12-in (30-cm) piece of heavy-duty foil and sprinkle with a pinch of salt and pepper. Set the onion, root-end down, in butter. Bring the ends of the foil together over the top of the onion and scrunch together. Place the onion on a medium grill and leave to cook for 45 minutes until tender. To serve, open the foil package and transfer the onion to a plate. Pour any remaining butter juices over the onion. You can cook several of these onion packages at the same time.

Seared lamb loin salad
Elegant

Every so often a "make-ahead" dish comes along that is not only effortless, but impressive as well. Thanks, I must admit, go to Sean Evans for many of my "impressive" tricks. This is my take on a recipe he culled from a year at cooking school in New Zealand. It's guaranteed to impress.

Serves 4

12oz (350g) **lamb loin**
Vegetable oil, for brushing

For the marinade:
2 **shallots**, thinly sliced
2 Tbsp **chopped mint**
2 Tbsp **chopped cilantro**
2 Tbsp **finely chopped fresh ginger**
1 **red finger chilli pepper**, deseeded and finely chopped
Juice and grated rind of 2 limes
2 tsp **fish sauce**
4 Tbsp **soy sauce**

For the salad:
5 cups (200g) **mixed salad leaves**
1 tsp **sesame oil**
Parmesan cheese shavings, to serve
Sea salt and pepper, to taste

Preheat the grill or grill pan to hot. Brush the lamb loin with oil and grill until a deep brown color, 2–3 minutes on all four sides. Allow to cool slightly.

Combine all the marinade ingredients in a shallow baking dish. Place the lamb in the marinade and turn to coat. Cover and refrigerate for 2–3 hours, turning occasionally. Remove the lamb from the marinade and thinly slice. Place the salad leaves in a bowl and toss with sesame oil and a spoonful of the lamb marinade. Place the salad on a serving platter and fan the sliced lamb on top. Scatter with Parmesan shavings and finish off with a sprinkling of sea salt and pepper and a drizzle of marinade.

Seared lamb loin salad

Desserts

Somewhere along the line, pleasure became synonymous with guilt. Many say it was an early puritanical trend, which has in some ways survived to this day.

This sense of guilt not only remains but it has woven its way into our culinary vernacular. Take desserts, for example. They are the ultimate in "guilty pleasures." Often they're variously described as "sinfully delicious," or "so bad they're good."

We think it's time to embrace such passions without guilt. Savoring is the secret. Most of us opt for junk food when we want a quick sweet fix, and more often than not it leaves us feeling unsatisfied and guilty. So enjoy the good stuff.

Grill those fresh, seasonal fruits. Bathe them in sweet cream. Sink your teeth into chocolate cream. Use your taste buds. It's real food, made by you in the garden. What's sinful about that?

Pineapple with coconut ice cream

Tropical

A scoop of homemade coconut ice cream served on hot, sweet and succulent pineapple slices.

Serves 4–6

For the ice cream:
1¼ cups (300ml) **whole milk**
2¼oz (60g) **creamed coconut**
¾ cup (100g) **confectioners sugar**
4 **large egg yolks**
½ cup (45g) **shredded coconut (optional)**
1¼ cups (300ml) **heavy cream**

1 **medium pineapple**, skin removed and cut into ½-in (1-cm) **thick slices**
Juice of 2 **limes**
Generous ½ cup (50g) **coconut flakes**
Mint sprigs, to serve

To make the ice cream, warm the milk in a saucepan to near-boiling point. Add the creamed coconut and stir until dissolved. Strain the warm coconut milk through a fine sieve. Beat the sugar and egg yolks in a heatproof bowl until thick and pale. Set the bowl over a pan of simmering water and gradually stir in the coconut milk. Stir occasionally until the mixture is thick enough to coat the back of a spoon. Stir in the shredded coconut, if using, and cool. Stir in the cream and churn in an ice-cream maker according to the manufacturer's instructions, until frozen. Pour into a freezer container, cover and freeze.

Take the ice cream out of the freezer 20 minutes before serving and preheat the grill or grill pan to medium. Brush the pineapple slices with lime juice and cook for 2–3 minutes on each side until dark golden and slightly softened. Serve 1–2 pineapple slices with scoops of ice cream, a sprinkling of coconut flakes and a mint sprig.

Mango cheeks with chilli syrup

Sticky

You've probably seen mango cheeks in every grill book you have ever owned, but serving them with this sticky, fiery syrup makes for a different dessert altogether.

Serves 2–4

Grated rind of 2 limes
4 Tbsp **extra-fine sugar**
2 **large mangos**

For the syrup:
½ cup (100g) **extra-fine sugar**
Scant ½ cup (100g) **water**
½ **red chilli,** halved and deseeded

Vanilla ice cream, to serve (optional)

Combine the lime rind and 4 Tbsp extra-fine sugar and spread evenly on a large flat plate. Cut the mango cheeks and sides from each mango, leaving the skin on. Criss-cross each piece into about ¾-in (2-cm) diamonds, but do not push out. Dip the cut side of the mangoes into the sugar and lime mixture, then turn flesh-side up and leave to rest until the sugar has dissolved – at least 20 minutes or up to 6 hours.

To make the syrup, combine the sugar, water and chilli. Bring to a boil and simmer for about 10 minutes. Sieve immediately, discarding the chilli, and leave to cool completely.

Heat the grill or grill pan to medium-hot. Brush any extra juices over the mango pieces and grill for 2–3 minutes flesh-side down, or until charred and starting to caramelize. Invert the mango cheeks and serve warm, with cooled chilli syrup poured over and vanilla ice cream on the side if liked.

Marsala-poached and grilled pears
Sophisticated

This is the perfect finish to any meal. Make sure you choose a creamy Gorgonzola and a sweet, sticky wine to have on the side. Bliss!

Serves 6

Generous 1 cup (250g)
   extra-fine sugar
Scant 1 cup (200ml) **Marsala**
1¼ cups (300ml) **water**
1 Tbsp **black peppercorns**
6 **Conference pears**, skin
   removed
7oz (200g) **Gorgonzola
   cheese**
1 cup (100g) **shelled
   walnut halves**, toasted

Put the sugar, Marsala, water and peppercorns in a large saucepan and bring to a boil over high heat, stirring until the sugar is dissolved. Add the pears and enough water to just cover them. Bring back to a boil, reduce the heat and simmer for about 20 minutes or until the pears are tender but still firm. Remove the pears and set aside. Bring the liquid back to a boil and leave to simmer until it has reduced to a syrup, about 45 minutes. Pour the syrup over the pears and leave to cool completely.

When you are ready to serve, preheat the grill pan to medium. Halve and core the pears and place cut-side down on the grill pan for 2–3 minutes or until the grill pan has left a decorative grill mark on them, then turn over and cook on the second side for a further 1–2 minutes. Remove from the pan and place two pear halves on each plate. Add a generous chunk of Gorgonzola on the side, sprinkle over the toasted walnuts and, finally, drizzle all over with the syrup. Serve immediately with some crisp crackers and a glass of Marsala or sweet dessert wine on the side, if liked.

Marsala-poached and grilled pears

Angel food cake with chocolate cream

Decadent

I'll never forget the day I first tasted grilled angel food cake with a dollop of chocolate cream. Nothing has really been the same since. Of course you can make your own cake if you prefer, but store-bought is the simple and guaranteed-to-be-fluffy option.

Serves 8

For the chocolate cream:
8 Tbsp **confectioners sugar**
4 Tbsp **cocoa powder**
2 Tbsp **milk**
1 cup (250ml) **heavy cream**
1 pinch **cream of tartar**

8 fat slices **store-bought angel food cake**
1–2 Tbsp **confectioners sugar,** for dusting

To make the chocolate cream, whisk together the confectioners sugar, cocoa powder and milk in a small bowl. Set aside. In a separate bowl, beat the cream with the cream of tartar until soft. Whisk in the chocolate mixture until well blended. Cover and refrigerate.

Preheat the grill or grill pan to hot. Dust the angel food cake slices with confectioners sugar. Grill the slices for 1 minute on each side until golden and grill marks appear on the surface. Transfer to serving plates and top with chocolate cream.

Grilled banana split

Grown-up

This is a quick, sophisticated way to serve up this diner-style dessert, topped with a delicious orange-caramel sauce. Who ever thought a banana split could be so posh?

Serves 4

For the sauce:
½ cup (100g) **sugar**
Generous ¼ cup (75ml) **water**
Generous ¼ cup (75ml) **heavy cream**
½ cup (125ml) **freshly squeezed orange juice**
1 tsp **grated orange rind**

For the grilled bananas:
2 **bananas,** skin removed and halved lengthways
Scant ¼ cup (30ml) **melted butter**
1 Tbsp **brown sugar**

2¼ cups (500ml) **vanilla ice cream**

To make the sauce, combine the sugar and water in a small saucepan over medium-low heat. Stir occasionally until sugar dissolves. Increase the heat and boil, gently, until the mixture darkens to a deep amber color, 6–8 minutes. Add the cream, orange juice and grated rind – the mixture will bubble vigorously. Reduce the heat and whisk constantly until smooth. Allow to cool. The sauce can be covered and refrigerated for up to 2 weeks.

Brush the banana halves with melted butter and sprinkle with brown sugar. Preheat the grill or grill pan to hot and brush the grill with oil. Grill the bananas on both sides, until warm and grill marks appear on the surface. Transfer to serving bowls. Top with ice cream and orange caramel sauce.

■ *Use blood oranges when in season.*

Grilled s'mores sandwiches

Gooey

Most North American children know the recipe for s'mores by heart: 1 campfire plus 1 roasted marshmallow sandwiched with a piece of chocolate between two graham crackers. It's a caramelized, charred, chocolatey heaven. Graham crackers don't fare well on the grill, however, so why not try brioche instead?

Serves 2

4 slices **brioche**
6 **large marshmallows**
3½oz (100g) **milk chocolate,** broken into chunks
Butter, softened

Preheat the grill or grill pan to medium-hot. Place the brioche slices on a cutting board. Divide the marshmallows between two pieces of brioche. Place the chocolate on top of the marshmallows. Top with the remaining brioche slices. Butter the top brioche slices.

Carefully invert the sandwiches onto the grill bars. Grill, pressing gently with a spatula, until the insides begin to melt and grill marks appear on the surface. Flip over, grill for a further minute, then transfer the sandwiches to a cooler part of the grill and continue to grill until the insides have completely melted, a further 1–2 minutes.

Transfer to plates and serve immediately.

■ *If brioche is unavailable, substitute another slightly sweet bread, such as Chollah.*

Grilled s'mores sandwiches

Roasted rhubarb with ginger syrup

Tart

Both barbecues and rhubarb are symbols of spring but, unfortunately, the two rarely meet. The union is simple and flavorsome and, like most barbecue recipes, the washing up is nil.

Serves 4

6 **stalks rhubarb, about** 1lb 5oz (600g),
    cut into 1½-in (4-cm) **lengths**
4 **pieces stem ginger,** finely chopped
4 Tbsp **stem ginger syrup**
Vanilla yogurt, ice cream or whipped cream, to serve

Preheat the grill to medium-hot, or preheat the oven to 350°F/180°C.

Take two sheets of foil, each 16-in (40-cm) long, and place one sheet on top of the other. Place the chopped rhubarb in the middle of the foil and toss with stem ginger and syrup. Bring the edges of the foil together and fold, creating an airtight package.

Place the foil package directly on the grill, cover and leave for 10–15 minutes until the rhubarb is cooked through. Spoon the rhubarb over vanilla yogurt, ice cream or simple whipped cream.

Roasted rhubarb with ginger syrup

Caramelized oranges on brioche

Caramelized oranges on brioche

Indulgent

This is a sweet version of bruschetta, and equally delicious. Brioche doesn't take long to toast so keep a close eye on it. Try using figs instead of oranges when they are in season.

Serves 4

4 **oranges,** skin removed and halved crosswise
2 Tbsp **unrefined brown sugar**
3 Tbsp **brandy**
4 **slices brioche**
Mint leaves, to serve (optional)

For the mascarpone cream:
Scant ½ cup (100g) **mascarpone**
Scant ½ cup (100g) **crème fraîche or sour cream**
½ cup (50g) **unrefined brown sugar**
1 tsp **vanilla extract**

Put the oranges in a flat dish, cut-side up. Sprinkle over the sugar. Drizzle over the brandy, cover and chill for 1–2 hours.

While the oranges are chilling, prepare the mascarpone cream. Combine all the ingredients in a bowl, mix until well combined and refrigerate until you are ready to serve, at least 1 hour.

Heat the grill hot plate (not grill plate) or grill pan to medium-hot and cook the brioche slices for about 30 seconds–1 minute on each side, or until just golden, and transfer to serving plates. Then cook the oranges, cut-side down, for about 4–5 minutes, pouring over the extra juices after 2–3 minutes. Move the oranges around in the syrup, turning once or twice, until dark brown, sticky and caramelized. Spread the mascarpone cream over the cooked brioche slices and top with the oranges and any juices. Serve warm with a mint leaf on top, if liked.

Accompaniments

Apricot BBQ sauce

Makes 6¼ cups (1.5L)

2lb 4oz (1kg) **ripe apricots,** halved and pitted
1lb 2oz (500g) **tomatoes,** halved
3½ cups (500g) **brown sugar**
2¼ cups (500ml) **cider vinegar**
2 **onions,** peeled and chopped

2 **cloves garlic**
1 **red chilli pepper,** halved
2 Tbsp **soy sauce**
2 tsp **Dijon mustard**
2 tsp **smoked paprika**

Put all the ingredients in a large saucepan or stockpot and mix to combine. Bring to a boil, reduce the heat and simmer for 1–1½ hours, or until thick and pulpy. Remove the chilli pepper and strain the sauce through a mouli-légumes or coarse sieve and pour into sterilized jars or bottles. This sauce will keep for up to 1 month. Refrigerate after opening.

Peanut sauce

Makes 2¼ cups (500ml)

1 Tbsp **peanut or groundnut oil**
1 **onion,** finely chopped
2 **cloves garlic,** crushed
½–1 tsp **chilli flakes**
2 Tbsp **dark soy sauce**

1 Tbsp **brown sugar**
1 Tbsp **tamarind paste or lime juice**
Scant 1 cup (200g) **crunchy peanut butter**
Scant 1 cup (200ml) **coconut milk**

Heat the oil in a medium saucepan and fry the onion, garlic and chilli flakes over medium heat for 3–4 minutes but do not brown. Reduce the heat to low and stir in the soy sauce, brown sugar, tamarind paste, peanut butter and coconut milk. Bring to a boil, reduce the heat and simmer for 2–3 minutes. This sauce will keep, covered, in the fridge for up to 1 week.

Gran's plum sauce

Makes 6¼ cups (1.5L)

3lb 5oz (1.5kg) **red plums**
1lb 10oz (750g) **brown sugar**
2 tsp **salt**
3 cups (750ml) **white wine vinegar**
1 tsp **cayenne pepper**

2 **onions**, chopped
2 **apples**, chopped
2 tsp **allspice**
1 tsp **ground cloves**
1-in (2.5-cm) piece **fresh ginger**, bruised

Put all the ingredients in a large saucepan and mix to combine. Bring to a boil, reduce the heat and simmer for 1½–2 hours, or until thick and pulpy. Strain the sauce through a mouli-légumes or coarse sieve and pour into sterilized jars or bottles. This sauce will keep for up to 1 month. Refrigerate after opening.

Sweet Thai chilli sauce

Makes 1½ cups (350ml)

4 **cloves garlic**, roughly chopped
2 large **red chilli peppers**, stems removed
2 tsp **grated fresh ginger**
Grated rind of 2 **limes**
2 stalks **lemongrass**, roughly chopped

½ cup (10g) **cilantro leaves and stalks**
1 cup (200g) **extra-fine sugar**
Generous ¼ cup (75ml) **cider vinegar**
3 Tbsp **fish sauce**
3 Tbsp **light soy sauce**

Purée the first six ingredients to a paste in a food processor. Put the sugar in a medium-sized saucepan with 3 Tbsp water and heat, stirring, until the sugar dissolves. Remove the spoon, increase the heat and boil gently for 5–6 minutes, until light golden caramel in color. Carefully stir in the paste. Bring back to a boil and add the vinegar, fish sauce and soy sauce. Bring back to a boil again and simmer for a further minute. Remove from the heat and leave to cool before serving. This sauce will keep for up to 1 month, stored in a sterilized, airtight jar in the fridge.

Mint sauce

Makes 1 scant cup (200ml)

4 cups (80g) mint, roughly chopped
2 Tbsp olive oil
Scant 1 cup (200ml) cider vinegar
Scant 1 cup (200ml) water
4 Tbsp extra-fine sugar

Put the mint and olive oil in a blender or food processor. Put the cider vinegar, water and sugar in a saucepan and bring to a boil. Reduce the heat and simmer for 10 minutes, or until halved in volume. Pour the hot liquid over the mint and blend briefly until combined. Remove and cool. This sauce can be refrigerated in a sterilized, airtight jar for up to 2 weeks.

Caramelized onions

1 Tbsp butter
1 Tbsp olive oil
2 large onions, sliced into ⅝-in (1.5-cm) rings
1 Tbsp balsamic vinegar
1 Tbsp brown sugar

Heat the butter and oil in a large frying pan over medium heat. Add the onions, stirring to coat. Sauté for 8–10 minutes, stirring occasionally, until softened and the edges begin to brown. Stir in the vinegar and sugar, cover and reduce the heat to low. Leave to cook slowly for 20–30 minutes, until the onions have collapsed and are meltingly tender.

Tzatziki

Makes 1 cup (250ml)

Scant 1 cup (200g) plain yogurt
½ large cucumber, deseeded and cut into small cubes
½ cup (10g) mint, shredded
Juice of 1 lemon
Salt and freshly ground black pepper

Combine all the ingredients in a bowl and refrigerate until ready to serve. This will keep in the refrigerator for 3–4 days.

Cranberry pear chutney

Makes 2½ cups (600ml)

¾ cup (180g) chopped shallots
1 Tbsp vegetable oil
12-oz (350-g) bag fresh or frozen cranberries
2 pears, peeled, cored, quartered and chopped

½ cup (120g) sugar
¼ cup (60ml) cider vinegar
1 tsp crushed garlic
1 tsp very finely chopped fresh ginger
½ tsp salt
½ tsp pepper

In a saucepan over medium heat sauté the shallots until softened, stirring often, about 10 minutes. Stir in the remaining ingredients and simmer, stirring occasionally, for 15 minutes, until the berries collapse. Store chutney in a sterilized, airtight jar or container for up to 2 weeks in the refrigerator or 3 months in the freezer.

Rosemary aïoli

Makes 1 cup (250ml)

3 large organic egg yolks
1–2 cloves garlic, crushed
2 Tbsp lemon juice
Generous ¼ cup (75ml) extra virgin
  olive oil

½ cup (125ml) vegetable oil
2 Tbsp finely chopped fresh rosemary
¼ tsp salt
Freshly ground black pepper, to taste

Whisk the egg yolks with the garlic and lemon juice until foamy. Slowly whisk in the oils in a thin stream, until mixture is thick and has emulsified. Whisk in rosemary, salt and pepper to taste. Cover and refrigerate until needed. Aïoli can be kept in the fridge for up to 2 days.

■ *This recipe uses raw egg. To minimize the risk of salmonella, children, pregnant women, the elderly and the sick should avoid raw eggs. Make sure to use only farm-fresh, organic eggs.*

Mustard bourbon BBQ sauce

Makes 3 generous cups (750ml)

1 tsp vegetable oil
1 bunch spring onions, chopped
1 medium onion, chopped
4 large cloves garlic, chopped
1¼ cups (200g) packed golden brown
  sugar
½ cup (125ml) tomato ketchup
¼ cup (75ml) tomato paste
½ cup (125ml) grainy Dijon mustard

½ cup (125ml) water
¼ cup (75ml) Worcestershire sauce
¼ cup (75ml) cider vinegar
¼ cup (75ml) apple juice
1 chipotle chilli in adobo sauce, finely
  chopped
1 tsp ground cumin
1½ cups (350ml) bourbon

Heat the oil in a heavy, large saucepan over medium-low heat. Add the spring onions, onion and garlic and sauté until tender, about 15 minutes. Mix in the remaining ingredients, adding the bourbon last. Simmer the sauce until thick and reduced to 3 generous cups (750ml), stirring occasionally, about 1 hour. Season to taste with salt and pepper. This sauce can be prepared 2 weeks ahead. Cover and refrigerate.

Flatbread

Makes 4 flatbread

2 tsp active dry yeast
Scant ½ cup (100ml) warm water
4½ cups (500g) plain flour
1½ tsp salt

1 Tbsp chopped rosemary, thyme or
  herb of choice
1 Tbsp extra virgin olive oil, for oiling
  the bowl
Scant 1 cup (200ml) carbonated water

Sprinkle the yeast over the warm water and leave for 5 minutes, or until foaming. Combine the flour, salt and chopped herbs in a large bowl and make a well in the center. Stir the yeast mixture and pour it into the well, with the olive oil and ⅔ cup (150ml) carbonated water. Draw the flour in from the sides, until it is all combined and adding extra water if needed. Knead the dough on a lightly floured surface for 10 minutes or until smooth and elastic. Put in a clean, oiled bowl and leave to rise for about 1½ hours or until doubled in size. Punch the dough down and leave for a further 10 minutes. Divide the dough into four and, on a lightly floured surface, roll out into rounds about 9in (23cm) in diameter and ¼-in (5-mm) thick. Cook for about 2–3 minutes on the first side, using a fork to prick any bubbles that form. Flip the bread over and cook for a further 2 minutes.

Pizza dough

Makes 6 8-in (20-cm) pizza crusts

2¼ tsp active dry yeast
1¼ cups (275ml) warm water
About 4½ cups (500g) plain flour

2 tsp salt
Generous ¼ cup (75ml) olive oil plus
  extra for oiling the bowl and brushing

Stir the yeast into the warm water, cover and let stand for 15 minutes until foaming. Combine the flour and salt in a large bowl. Slowly add the yeast mixture and olive oil alternately, stirring after each addition. Turn the dough out on to a lightly floured work surface and knead for 8 minutes until the dough is soft and elastic. Place the dough in a big, lightly oiled bowl and leave to rise until doubled in size, about 1 hour.

Punch down the dough and divide into six balls. Flatten and shape them into circles, cover with plastic wrap and leave to rest for 5 minutes. Shape the circles again so they are 8in (20cm) in diameter. Brush with oil and grill for 2–3 minutes. Flip the dough over and add your pizza toppings on the cooked side. Brown the bottom of the dough.

Glossary

Aïoli – A raw egg, crushed garlic and olive oil emulsion. The result is a smooth, creamy, sharp sauce similar to mayonnaise.

Banana leaf – A faintly smoky and lightly fragrant leaf used to wrap foods, either for presentation or to protect while cooking. Banana leaves are traditionally used where bananas are grown, but are readily available in Asian food markets.

Baste – To brush with sauce during the cooking process.

Beef tomatoes – Large, bright red and slightly elliptical in shape, beef tomatoes are highly flavored.

Bibb/Boston/round lettuce – Members of the butterhead family, which have buttery, not crisp, round leaves. The flavor is sweet and the leaves are delicate and tender.

Bok choy – A mild Chinese cabbage with dark, leafy tops and white, crisp stalks.

Chicory – Chicory has long, crispy, bitter-tasting leaves. It is good in salads, or the whole head can be braised. Also called endive and witlof.

Chimichurri – A fresh herb and vinegar mixture used in Argentinean cookery, either to baste grilled meats or as a condiment.

Chipolatas – Small sausages usually stuffed with pork, herbs and cooked rice.

Chorizo – Spicy Spanish or Mexican pork sausages flavored with garlic and chilli powder. Chorizo is usually made with fresh pork in Mexico and smoked pork in Spain.

Crayfish/lobster – Crayfish are freshwater crustaceans, while lobsters are marine crustaceans. Both vary greatly in size, but are similar in taste and texture.

Creamed coconut – Made by combining one part water to four parts shredded coconut, simmered, then strained. It is sold as a thick block wrapped in plastic and packaged in a cardboard box.

Crème fraîche – A thickened cream, thicker than sour cream, with a tangy, nutty flavor. You can make your own by combining 1 cup (250ml) double cream with 2 Tbsp buttermilk. Cover and allow to stand for 8–24 hours until very thick. Stir well, then refrigerate for up to 10 days.

Finger chilli – A long, slender green or red chilli usually up to 4in (10cm) in length. Medium-hot on the temperature scale.

Fingerling potatoes – A small potato, with a creamy, moist center. Fingerlings are ideal for roasting, parboiling and grilling.

Fish sauce – A Southeast Asian condiment made from salted fermented fish, used to salt dishes. The Thai version is called *nam pla*, while the Vietnamese call it *nuoc nam*.

Five-spice powder – A pungent and aromatic blend of Chinese spices, made up of star anise, cloves, fennel seeds, cinnamon and Szechuan peppercorns.

Garam masala – A spice mixture used in Indian and Middle Eastern dishes. Often a mixture of cumin, cloves, cinnamon, cardamom, nutmeg and pepper.

Gorgonzola – A creamy, blue cheese named after the Italian village of Gorgonzola, near Milan, where it was first made.

Halloumi – A firm, salty sheep's cheese commonly used as a cooking cheese in Middle Eastern countries.

Julienne – To slice finely into matchstick shapes.

Kaffir lime leaves – The leaves of an evergreen native to Southeast Asia. The zest of the limes and leaves of this tree have a fresh, citrus-floral flavor.

Kecap manis – A thick, sweet dark soy sauce of Indonesian origin. Available from Asian markets.

Marsala – A rich, smoky, fortified wine from Sicily ranging from sweet to dry.

Mirin – Like Chinese rice wine, mirin is a Japanese low-alcohol, sweet golden wine made from glutinous rice. It adds a distinctive sweetness to dishes.

Miso paste – Miso, or bean paste, is a staple in Japanese cooking. It is fermented soybean paste that looks rather like peanut butter. Three categories of miso paste are available: barley miso, rice miso and soybean miso. All are injected with a mould then aged from 6 months to 3 years. The flavor depends on the amount of mould injected, the amount of salt used and the period of fermentation.

Palm sugar – This dark, coarse, unrefined sugar, also known as jaggery, can be made either from the sap of palm trees or from sugar-cane juice. Primarily used in Southeast Asia, it comes in several forms, the two most popular being a soft, honey-butter texture and a solid cake-like form.

Polenta – A staple dish in Italy made from cornmeal. To make polenta, cornmeal is boiled in water and then simmered until thick. Polenta can be served warm or spread into a thin layer, cooled then cut and reheated by grilling, frying or baking.

Pomegranate syrup/molasses – A syrup made from the juices of sour, not sweet, pomegranate seeds. The juice is boiled down to a thick syrup, and used often in Iranian cooking.

Porcini mushrooms – With their meaty texture, fine flavor and distinctive shape, these Italian mushrooms are expensive but worth it. Look for them fresh, when in season, or dried throughout the year.

Poultry shears – Heavy-duty kitchen scissors essential for butchering poultry and other fowl.

Quark – A fresh curd cheese made from skim milk.

Sear – To cook an ingredient over very high heat to form a seal which traps moisture within.

Sumac – A berry that grows on a shrub native to Iran. The berries are ground and sprinkled over foods to add an acidic flavor, in the way lemon or tamarind is used. Sumac is also said to bring out the flavors in other foods, as salt does.

Tamarind – The fruit of a shade tree native to Asia. The large pods contain a sweet-sour pulp that is especially sour when dried. It is used to season many East Indian, Asian and Middle Eastern dishes, in the way lemon juice is used. Sold as a juice, paste or dried and ground into powder.

Tortillas – Unleavened, flat bread from Mexico made either from corn or wheat flour.

about the authors

Pippa Cuthbert is a New Zealander living and working in London. Ever since childhood she has been passionate about food and cooking. After studying Nutrition and Food Science at Otago University in New Zealand and working in the test kitchen of Nestlé New Zealand, she decided to travel the world in search of new and exciting culinary adventures. Now based in London, Pippa works as a food writer and stylist on books and magazines, and is also involved in advertising and commercials.

Food and writing are **Lindsay Cameron Wilson's** passions, so she blended the two at university where she studied History, Journalism, and the Culinary Arts. She has since worked in the test kitchens of *Canadian Living Magazine* in Toronto and *Sunset Magazine* in San Francisco. In 2001 she left her job as a food columnist in Halifax, Nova Scotia, and moved to London. That's when she met Pippa, and the work for their first book, *Juice!* began. Fuelled by juice, the two moved on to *Ice Cream!*, *Soup!* and now *Barbecue!* Lindsay continues to work as a food journalist in Canada, where she now lives with her husband, James, and son, Luke.

Index